SOMETHING IS MISSING
THINGS WE DON'T WANT TO KNOW
ABOUT LOVE, SEX AND LIFE

What a joy! Bülent Somay's new-old text, translated from the Turkish by Bülent himself, takes us into the impenetrable heart of obscure Lacanian psychoanalysis and comes out with clarity, wit and epithetical precision. Theory comes alive here; and along with the fun and games, something dark is brought into the light.

- Stephen Frosh, author of Feelings, Psychoanalysis Outside the Clinic, Hauntings and Those Who Come After)

With clarity, wit and copious erudition, Bülent Somay brings his critical psychoanalytic eye to our most challenging human relations – the tribulations of sex, love and desire. Somay's committed sexual politics informs this essential addition to our knowledge of the pleasures and perils of the bonds of desire. *Something is Missing* is not to be missed.

- Lynne Segal, author of Radical Happiness: Moments of Collective Joy.

For Ezgi,
then and now

There is a crack, a crack in everything
That's how the light gets in

Leonard Cohen, Anthem

SOMETHING IS MISSING

THINGS WE DON'T WANT TO KNOW ABOUT LOVE, SEX AND LIFE

Bülent Somay

TRANSNATIONAL PRESS LONDON

2021

SOCIETY AND POLITICS: 5

Something is Missing - Things We don't Want to Know about Love, Sex and Life

Bülent Somay

Copyright © 2021 Transnational Press London

All rights reserved. This book or any portion thereof may not be reproduced or used in any manner whatsoever without the express written permission of the publisher except for the use of brief quotations in a book review or scholarly journal.

First Published in English 2021 by TRANSNATIONAL PRESS LONDON in the United Kingdom, 12 Ridgeway Gardens, London, N6 5XR, UK. Translated into English by the author from the original Turkish version which was published by Metis Publishers in 2007.
www.tplondon.com

Transnational Press London® and the logo and its affiliated brands are registered trademarks.

Requests for permission to reproduce material from this work should be sent to: sales@tplondon.com

Paperback
ISBN: 978-1-912997-86-2

Digital
ISBN: 978-1-80135-026-6

Cover Design: Nihal Yazgan
Cover Photo: "Lack Old Leather Seat. Broken Leather" by tighofur, photo ID: 1613495344, https://www.shutterstock.com/image-photo/lack-old-leather-seat-broken-1613495344

CONTENTS

About the Author 1

Preface 3

Introduction: Things We Don't Want To Know About Love, Sex And Life 7

Chapter 1. Something is Missing 19

Chapter 2. Knight in Shining Armour 29

Chapter 3. Jealous of You I Am 39

Chapter 4. That Dark/Obscure Object of Desire 51

Chapter 5. 'There is No Such Thing As A Sexual Relationship' ... 61

Chapter 6. ~~The Wo~~man Does Not Exist Anyhow 71

Chapter 7. *Silentium Universi* 83

Chapter 8. The Truth is Out There/'The Real' is Out There Somewhere .. 93

Index 103

ABOUT THE AUTHOR

Bülent Somay is born in Istanbul and has BA and MA degrees in English Language and Literature, and holds a PhD in Psychosocial Studies. He was a Lecturer in Comparative Literature and Cultural Studies in Istanbul Bilgi University between 2000 and 2017. He has published seven books in Turkish (*Cinselliğe Dair Vazgeçmemiz Gereken Yüz Efsane* [A Hundred Myths on Sexuality We Need to Give Up], 2016; *Tarih, Otobiyografi ve Hakikat* [History, Autobiography and Truth], 2015, ed.; *Çokbilmiş Özne* [The Subject Who Knows Too Much], 2008; *Bir Şeyler Eksik* [Something is Missing], 2007; *Tarihin Bilinçdışı* [The Unconscious of History], 2004; *Şarkı Okuma Kitabı* [Song Reader], 2000; *Geriye Kalan Devrimdir* [What Remains is the Revolution], 1997), and two books in English (*The View from the Masthead*, 2010; *The Psychopolitics of the Oriental Father*, 2014). His most recent publication is 'The Three-Mother Problem' in the October 2019 issue of *Journal of Psychosocial Studies*. He is recently living in exile as an Academy in Exile fellow in Freie Universität, Berlin.

PREFACE

These essays (aphorisms, theses, whatever you like) were written fifteen years ago in Turkish, and were published in Turkey in 2007.[1] It was almost an idyllic, Arcadian time if considered from the point of view of today, that is, the nightmarish year 2020 when I am writing this. Trump was still your run-of-the-mill Reality TV star (who was also a millionaire), and could harm only his immediate environment. We only had to deal with the common cold and the flu, which, although deadly enough, could not even begin to compete with the Covid-19 pandemic. Turkey, Russia and India were ruled by populists with authoritarian tendencies even then; but their rule did not seem as eternal and as aggressively autocratic, bordering on fascism, as it is today. We could still say, 'Capitalism will be capitalism!' and make plans and organise for its downfall and aftermath, rather than focus all our strength just to survive, as we are doing today. I was teaching in a decent enough university then, but now I am living in voluntary exile, just because I signed a petition for peace!

Since then, the book was reprinted eight times in Turkish, with no changes made whatsoever, which was a thorn in my side, since the world was rapidly changing, maybe faster than ever, especially in the last five years. In translation, which I did myself, these essays were updated, 'upgraded', expanded and sometimes entirely rewritten, to retain whatever relevance they had, and also to keep up and develop with the times, although they were not related to the 'current affairs' *per se*, but seemingly mostly 'theoretical'.

My main objective was to comment rather freely on how psychoanalysis can be a consequential means to comprehend and, if possible, change our daily lives for the better (a rather 'philosophical' task), to question our ready-made and supposedly self-evident ideas and positions on love, sex and a better life, or *eudaimonia*. In doing so, I tried to adopt a Nietzschean form (especially the formal characteristics of *Die Fröhliche Wissenchaft* (Gay Science, [1882]), and partially the aphorismatic style of Adam Phillips' *Monogamy* (1996). At that time, I was also quite persuaded by Žižek's early attempts to re-narrate Lacan 'through popular culture' (especially in *Looking Awry* [1991] and *Enjoy Your Symptom!* [1992]), in order to make Lacanian arguments, which were usually quite opaque for people not well-versed in psychoanalysis and/or continental philosophy and/or linguistics and semiotics (most of the time all of them), more accessible to people outside a small, close-knit and elite community of

---

[1] *Bir Şeyler Eksik*; ©Metis Publishers, Istanbul, 2007. Translated and printed by permission from the publishers.

scholars and analysts.

What I managed to write in the end, however, was not a 'Lacan for Beginners', as I secretly feared I would have done, and, thankfully, not another opaque and 'academic' treatise on Lacan either. I had hoped to strike an equilibrium between the radicalism of a 'ruthless criticism of all that exists' and the empathetic endeavour of thinking from the 'other' point of view, an equilibrium that I have elsewhere called 'radical ambiguity'[2]. A peculiar combination of the Brechtian *Verfremdungseffect* and the literary equivalent of the Daoist dictum, Compassion, Moderation, Modesty. When I went over the book fifteen years later as a translator, I was moderately pleased to see that I had not failed miserably in this task.

Why an English version? Other than the selfish and covertly (or maybe overtly, I may not be fooling anybody) narcissistic desire to 'reach audiences everywhere', I have a more 'conscious' and deliberate intention: I sincerely believe that psychoanalytic thinking can properly function as a *Weltanschauung*, only by becoming polyglot, addressing 'the matter at hand' from the perspectives of different languages and cultures. Since it is predicated upon the fundamental presupposition that our actions, thoughts, emotions and behaviour originate in unconscious as well as conscious processes, psychoanalysis cannot operate well accepting the delimitations of a single language, a single symbolic order. 'The Unconscious is structured like a language,' said Lacan.[3] This means, among a lot of other things, it *matters* in which language you are thinking and writing on the 'unconscious', because every language has a different history and structure, and these differences reflect upon *what* you think and *how* you express these thoughts, even though you are not aware of it.

The more languages you are acquainted with, the more your horizon in psychoanalysis stretches and expands. The more psychoanalytical basic texts were translated into languages other than their 'original' language, German, and the more original psychoanalytical contributions were made in other languages, the more the scope of psychoanalysis broadened. Take, for instance, one of the most fundamental psychoanalytical concepts, 'the ego': in its original German, it was '*das Ich*', simply 'the I'. When it was being translated into French, however, it took a long time for French analysts and linguists to decide whether it should be '*le Moi*' or '*le Je*', finally deciding on '*le Moi*'. In English, Freud's translators preferred the Latin '*ego*' over 'I' for various reasons that I have neither the time nor the desire to go into here.

---

[2] Cf. my 'On Radical Ambiguity' in *The End of Truth: Five Essays on the Demise of Neoliberalism* (Forthcoming in 2021). London: Transnational Press.
[3] Jacques Lacan, The Seminar of Jacques Lacan Book XI: The Four Fundamental Concepts of Psychoanalysis;
Ed. Jacques-Alain Miller, Tr. Alan Sheridan; New York & London: W. W. Norton & Company, 20.

Whatever the reasons, the French and English concepts had a variety and abundance of connotations different from '*das Ich*', which complicated, but at the same time enriched and extended the psychoanalytical paradigm.

This is why I keep many allusions to Turkish culture and language I used in the original Turkish text in this English rendering: although not many (some, definitely, but not *enough*) contributions have been made to the entirety of the psychoanalytical pool of concepts and arguments by Turkophone thinkers and practitioners, the language and the culture themselves offer many paths to broaden its horizons. Take, for instance, *vuslat* (وصلة), an Arabic/Turkish word I occasionally use in the English text (2.20, 2.32, 2.40, 4.33). It comes from the Arabic root, *wṣl*, which means 'arrival', 'union' or 'meeting'. It is primarily used in Turkish literature for '(re)union with the beloved' since at least 1330 CE, almost all the time negatively, as something unreachable, something that failed to happen, a missed opportunity, a sad impossibility, a sorrowful ending. As such, it is a perfect term to denote the impossibility of the 'satisfaction' of (a) desire, which has no single-word equivalent in European languages, but only lengthy descriptions.

Another such word (not in Turkish this time, but Classical Hebrew and Aramaic) is '*yada*' (ידע), which means both 'to know' and 'to have sexual intercourse with', which is used as such in the Old Testament hundreds of times. The term has been taken over by American popular culture, e.g. in the TV show *Seinfeld*, where the characters often use it as '*Yada, yada, yada!*', which has two different connotations, one 'Blah, blah, blah!', but the other, more tacit one, 'They had sex!'. It is also referred to, again in popular culture, humorously, as '*Knew*, you know, Biblically!' As such, it refers to the often-neglected link between knowledge and desire, and also to the non-sexual usage of 'desire' as well as the sexual connotations of the *will to know*, something that can only be expressed in roundabout ways in many modern languages.

So, here are 346 aphorisms (or theses), or eight essays if you prefer it that way, trying to address the relevance of psychoanalysis, not as a technique of individual therapy, which I leave to qualified analysts who have the patience, training and temperament, but as a world outlook which may help in understanding and improving our lives. At times they become self-reflexive and try to comment on themselves, so far as it is possible. At times they (may) become, or come close to, the know-all grouching of somebody who mistakes his own experiences for 'reality' (Groucho Marx is one of my favourite heroes after all), for which I hope you will forgive me, because I hope there are enough self-reflexive arguments to counterbalance these. My own basic premise, after all, is that 'Something is Missing' all the time, in everything we do, and what good is an argument which does not occasionally turn around and shoot itself in the foot?

INTRODUCTION: THINGS WE DON'T WANT TO KNOW ABOUT LOVE, SEX AND LIFE

> 42.
>
> Douglas Adams, Life, the Universe and Everything

I'm not sure what this book really is. There's no doubt it is a book of essays, but it moves away from it from time to time to experiment in a more 'academic' mode. Stylistically, it's also a book of aphorisms. But let's not automatically assume that every paragraph beginning with a number is an aphorism; some numbered paragraphs (as should not be done in the form of 'aphorisms') are connected to the paragraphs preceding and following them, turning them into syllogisms with a logical sequence that can be meaningful only when considered together. It is not a book of theses either; if I had so many (346) 'theses', I would have to write not one but ten books, and most of them would mainly be full of empty drivel. So, the book you have in hand is a book of essays that is structured as aphorisms, in which you can occasionally come across some theses. If I had some hope that this (maybe unnecessarily) complex form would take hold, I would even make up a stylish name for it, but I don't think it's worth it.

This is not a book about psychoanalysis; indeed, apart from a few titles, subtitles and quotations, it does not progress with references and discussions from psychoanalytic theory. On the contrary, it tries to provide clues as to how we can utilise a psychoanalytic outlook in everyday life. That is why one of the punctuation marks it uses the most is the question mark. Because it suggests that psychoanalysis is not a technique to provide answers/solutions, but a way of asking questions, hopefully the correct questions (if there is such a thing), contrary to what contemporary pop-psychology and pop-psychiatry insistently imply. I cannot emphasise the importance of this difference enough: Psychoanalysis does not give us answers, it does not offer us solutions; because in order to do that, the person who applies it, the psychoanalyst, has to assume that they know all the right answers. The analyst, however, is just a person like us, their only advantage being specific knowledge about psychoanalytic technique. They have, however, no idea (more than any one of us) on entirely ethical/philosophical issues such as right and wrong or true and false. Otherwise they would not be psychoanalysts, but experts on Truth.

What Does Psychoanalysis Analyse?

There's also a practical reason why I'm insistent on this emphasis: recently, disciplines such as psychology, psychiatry and psychoanalysis (essentially different from one another) have evolved into 'popular' areas, as a result of considerable effort from mainstream, as well as 'social', media. Scarcely a day goes by without an 'expert' appearing on television or in newspapers, or on Twitter or Facebook, and comment on what 'caused' a suicide, 'why' another was depressed, 'why' someone else committed a murder, or became a Satanist, or beat his girlfriend. One of these 'media experts' explains the meaning and necessity of psychotherapy as follows:

> Psychotherapy is the method used to eliminate mental problems or behavioural disorders. Psychotherapy is based on the patient's conversations with the physician. The patient describes his childhood, past traumas, negative habits, emotional conflicts. Here psychotherapy resolves these conflicts, reduces anxiety and tensions, the level of spiritual harmony increases. These dialogue sessions can make the person and the development process aware of the obstacles that stand in the way. Individual therapy sessions usually last 40-45 minutes. Psychotherapy, in its simplest and most understandable form, is the replacement of the feelings and thoughts that operate erroneously in the brain-computer, by a specialist with the correct result, that is, the correct behaviour.[1]

I do not lightly refer to this approach, published in a daily newspaper (hence extremely volatile and temporary), albeit by a fairly famous and 'well-respected' psychiatrist in Turkey. The quote is sixteen years old, but the 'expert' is still famous and well-respected, now also on social media with a vengeance, and he still seems to be insistent on the opinion he expressed here. This opinion is worth mentioning not only because these words are very significant on their own, but also because they represent the pop-'psychology-psychiatry-psychoanalysis' triangle in vogue, not only in Turkey, but also all around the world for the last decades. The first thing we understand from the paragraph above is that it is possible to 'eliminate' mental problems or behavioural disorders. Although the practice of psychoanalysis tells us that some behavioural disorders are 'reparable' to a definite extent, it does not suggest or make a claim that 'mental problems', that is, personality traits/disorders, neuroses and especially psychoses, can be 'eliminated'. The best thing psychotherapy can offer in these situations is that it is possible to learn to cope with these 'problems' or, at most, to coexist with them more or less peacefully.

The greatest problem with this approach, however, is not simply that. Our expert gives us a definition of psychotherapy, as 'the replacement of feelings

---

[1] Dr. Arif Verimli, *Radikal* Daily Newspaper, September 1, 2006, my translation: http://www.radikal.com.tr/hayat/depresyon-ve-panik-atak-6-790439/.

and thoughts that operate erroneously in the brain-computer, by a specialist with the correct result, that is, the correct behaviour.' I will not comment on the downsides of the brain-computer metaphor, the brain being compared to a computer (i.e. a human-made machine), because almost everyone uses this metaphor from time to time although they very well know its drawbacks. The problem here is rather 'the replacement of feelings and thoughts that operate erroneously' by—what? The correct ones! And by 'an expert', no less. What is the area of 'expertise' of this person, one is bound to ask. First, they should be experts on how to change the feelings and thoughts in the brain, how to manipulate them, because as we all know from our everyday lives that it is no mean feat. It is extremely difficult to change the feelings and thoughts of individuals even in issues such as simple everyday local politics, or the football team they support, let alone their unconscious characteristics. These psychotherapy specialists, then, are supposed to be 'experts in mental manipulation'.

But this is not all. Not only do they need to be experts in manipulation, they should also be experts on what 'correct' is. When you seek help from a psychotherapist, therefore, you should also be prepared to embrace their opinion of 'correctness'. If I, for instance, went to an 'expert', wearing my long hair and beard, say, complaining of depression, I may be coming out of their door my hair cut and my beard shaved, wearing a three-piece suit, because that expert may simply believe that it is the 'correct' attire for a man of my age and stature, without listening to any arguments to the contrary. Who am I to know (or pretend to know) otherwise? And what difference will it make if I try to persist in my opinion (and in my own body-image) anyway? That psychotherapy specialist is an 'expert in mental manipulation', and I *am going to* change, whether I like it or not.

I'm not going to go into the subtle (and sometimes not-so-subtle) differences between the disciplines that take the 'psycho' (soul/mind) prefix. Regardless of their names, however, if the people who practice these disciplines essentially adopt a despotic mindset and believe that the few common truisms they have learned here and there throughout their lives represent a universal 'Truth', there will be a serious amount of bullying and coercion in the name of psychiatry, psychology and psychoanalysis. I don't pretend to speak for the other two, but personally I don't want to be a silent witness to psychoanalysis falling victim to this power-play. Psychoanalysis (or any person operating under the title 'psychoanalyst') does not know 'the Truth'; they can only help us in our pursuit for it. But if some psychoanalysts try to impose upon us their own 'truths', this is not the fault of psychoanalysis. If the same people were in politics, they would have called facts that don't agree with them 'Fake news!' and consistently complain about either the ignorance or the 'elitism' of anybody who opposed them. If they were in a loosely connected 'scientific' field, they would call the impending environmental catastrophe an 'exaggeration' and 'political bias' on the part of other scientists. Just as we can't rightfully say that politics in general is essentially despotic and bogus because of these politicians, or 'science' is the trumped-up (pun intended) declarations of these self-proclaimed 'scientists', neither can we say that psychoanalysis is a bully *in itself*: it is just that *some psychoanalysts are*.

Once we establish this, I can now argue that psychoanalysis does have something very important to say about our lives.

Psychoanalysis and Truth

One of the things I will insistently suggest throughout this book, maybe the most important one, is that there does not exist a knowable, conceivable Truth, neither is there an 'A-ha!' or 'Eureka!' moment for it. The limits of this claim itself, however, should be acknowledged and its relationship with its own 'Truth' needs to be established as well. Stanislaw Lem said, back in 1972 that:

> I should wish, as do most men, that immutable truths existed, that not all would be eroded by the impact of historical time, that there were some essential propositions, be it only in the field of human values, the basic values, etc. In brief, I long for the absolute. But at the same time I am firmly convinced that there are no absolutes, that everything is historical, and that you cannot get away from history.[2]

Just because there's no accessible truth as such does not mean that we should give up the effort to attain it, to reach for it. This sentence may seem paradoxical, so we should discuss it in a little more detail: In the postmodern age, truth has become something 'relative' and negotiable. There is an upside as well as a downside to this. Enlightenment belief systems, which endured until mid-twentieth century (in both their rationalistic and positivist incarnations), preached a unique truth that could be objectively identified. Postmodern belief systems opposed this and made the truth into something *relative*. Instead of an objective and absolute Truth, they talked about an infinite series of qualified, plural and virtual truths that every thought system, every method, and eventually every individual can achieve (or ignore) on their own. The common (social or communal, voluntary or reluctant) forms of behaviour were a product of the consensuses that would be achieved through negotiation among this multitude of truths. Thus, in the wake of

---

[2] 'Don't Believe Everything That You Know About Lem' (interview with Lem), *Nurt* #8 (1972); cited in **Jerzy Jarzębski, 'Stanislaw Lem, Rationalist and Visionary'; Science** Fiction Studies # 12 = Volume 4, Part 2 = July 1977; https://www.depauw.edu/sfs/backissues/12/jarzebski12.htm.

commodities, thoughts, emotions, beliefs and art, the Truth also became a part of the free market economy: we owe this development to postmodernism, which represents the final stage of capitalism (as far as we know it)[3].

Postmodernism saved the truth from its absolute position, but on the other hand, it commodified it, making it an object of bargain and trade. Come to think of it, however, this is not something to fret about. It is not very different from what capitalism had been doing for three centuries after all. During the 17th and 18th centuries, and especially throughout the Enlightenment, capitalism needed an absolute and universal truth—when it was unicentral, that is, exclusively European. Globalising/Globalised capitalism, on the other hand, adopted the dynamics of postmodernism, even before it became a school of thought *as such*, which subjectivised and dispersed truth, because it realized that it should be multi-cultural and hence capable of addressing more than one policy of truth.[4] Clinging to the idea of an enlightening/universalist/ absolutist (but still capitalist) truth of the previous century, therefore, will surely create an opposition to the postmodern market-truth, but this opposition can only create a reactionary/regressive agenda rather than a revolutionary one.

Psychoanalysis, as Adam Phillips points out, occupies the middle-ground, or, better yet, is in a kind of pendulum motion, between enlightenment universalism and postmodernist relativism. This is why, Phillips says, we can perceive Freud in two different ways, as 'Enlightenment Freud' and 'Post-Freudian' Freud.[5] These two aspects of Freud are not chronologically discernible or exactly sequential. On the contrary, these two aspects were always co-existent at different times in Freud's thinking, with varying significance. Psychoanalysis not only contains the consistent search for a truth which is the most positive aspect of the Enlightenment, that is, freedom from dogmas and 'given' facts; but it also bears the kernel of an understanding that problematises the existence of an attainable and transmissible universal truth, an understanding which will develop in the second half of the twentieth century. In short, psychoanalysis tries to make sense of not only 'unhealthy' behaviours and symptoms, but *all* our behaviours, thoughts and emotions by establishing a series of causal connections. In doing this, it also acknowledges that these behaviours, thoughts and emotions can never be explained in their entirety because they

---

[3] Accordingly, Fredric Jameson named his 1991 book, *Postmodernism, or, the Cultural Logic of Late Capitalism* (Durham, NC: Duke University Press), although the article of the same name which served as the foundation stone of the book was published much earlier, in 1984 (New Left Review, I/146, July/Aug 1984).

[4] Cf. my 'On Radical Ambiguity' and 'The End of Truth As We Know It: The Disintegration of University Discourse' in *The End of Truth: Five Essays on the Demise of Neoliberalism* (Forthcoming in 2021). London: Transnational Press London.

[5] Adam Phillips (1997). *Terrors and Experts*, Boston, MA: Harvard University Press, 1-17, *passim*.

are always over-determined (*surdéterminé*), and have a kernel that escapes our endeavours for an explanation, rationalisation and signification.

When we appeal to psychoanalysis, therefore, as an effort to understand/make sense of our lives, we know that we should not stop looking for this truth, even if we do not hope that we will achieve a universal Truth, or rather actually freeze and absolutise the moment we assume that we have reached this truth, at some point in our search. What is important in psychoanalysis is the search itself, the effort to *make sense*, in both senses of the term: both to *find* a meaning in, and to *make*, to *construct* a meaning out of the seemingly chaotic events that make up our lives. Consequently, we will not find any ultimate solutions in psychoanalytic therapy (or in any psychoanalytic endeavour of signification); a magic wand that will fix this or that symptom in a moment, or immediately 'correct' a personality disorder; it is the therapy process itself that is significant.

I have no claim (nor the temperament or the training) to be a therapist: what I'm trying to do here is to take examples of the artistic and cultural products of a certain age, the more 'popular' the better since these latter occupy a larger space in our daily lives, and examine them with a more or less 'psychoanalytic' method of scrutiny. This effort, however, just like the psychoanalytic therapy process itself, can only have a value in the process itself rather than its results. What matters is *how* I arrive at results, rather than results themselves; *which steps of signification* I go through, rather than which meanings or connotations I ascribe to a metaphor or a given text.

Let us take an example that I will focus upon in detail further on: it does not change anything that Buñuel later claimed that the fact that the same role was played by two separate actors in *Cet obscur objet du désir* (That Dark/Obscure Object of Desire), did not have any specific meaning, that it was a simple necessity because an actor had left the production in the middle of the shooting.[6] We can still try to find a meaning, an underlying significance in this fact, even if the author/director had not intended it, or denies having intended it. Because our endeavour to make sense of it or to find a specific meaning in it, was not a claim to reveal the 'truth' of the film in the first place.

What really matters is which paths this effort to make sense takes, which conceptual connections it makes, what kind of an understanding it offers on 'Desire', based on that specific situation. And finally, we should question what impact this effort, the connections it establishes, and the propositions it puts forward, makes on our lives and on our ideas about our existence. The rest does not matter much. That's why how a text (a novel, a poem, a film, a political manifesto) is interpreted by its author/director, does not occupy the

---

[6] In fact, this revelation makes the fact all the more 'obscure', because the actor he names to have abandoned the production is *Maria Schneider*, who is not in the final version of the film at all.

centre stage in our effort to make sense of it. Because what we're really searching for in it is not the truth of that text itself (craftily designed and embedded in it by the author), but *our own truth*.

This does not mean that I am suggesting an approach like, 'If the truth is so subjective, then we can make it up as we please!' Quite to the contrary, the truths we discover about ourselves while we are pursuing for meaning in texts, are fundamentally the prerequisite for communicating with each other, finding common concerns, and finally creating common areas of activity and action. Truths that can make an impact in practice arise and are made sense of not in revelations and divine inspirations, or in the minds of gifted/brilliant/sainted individuals, but rather in the interaction between ordinary individuals, the readers, the audiences. That's why the more we doubt the existence, comprehensibility and transmissibility of an absolute, single and objective *Truth*, the more we're going to redouble our efforts to seek *truth*, as the conceptualisation of what may have happened and what is yet to come.

You may ask how this is different from the postmodern/relativistic conception of 'truth' that I have been criticising above. There's a fundamental *temporal* or sequential difference between 'postmodernist' relativism and what I'm trying to suggest right now. In the postmodern belief system, or at least in its crudest version, the subject arrives at the truth *first on its own*, and then consensuses are sought and reached among these subjects through discussion and negotiation, most of them amounting to little more than 'agree to disagree'. What I propose, however, is just the opposite: Truth can come into being only in the inter-subjective space. Individualization is in the community itself; the result is in the (re)search; the object of desire is the product of the quest; objectivity arises from the interaction of subjects. In 1844, Marx and Engels suggested in *The German Ideology,* that:

> Man is in the most literal sense of the word a *zoon politikon*, not only a social animal, but an animal which can develop into an individual only in society. Production by isolated individuals outside of society —something which might happen as an exception to a civilized man who by accident got into the wilderness and already dynamically possessed within himself the forces of society— is as great an absurdity as the idea of the development of language without individuals living together and talking to one another.[7]

Subjects only become individuals *within* society, who establish constantly changing relationships with each other and create (again, incessantly changing) objectivities through these relationships. There is, of course, a

---

[7] Marx & Engels (1998). *The German Ideology*, Amherst, NY: Prometheus Books, 2.

'Reality' that existed *before* these subjects, and will go on existing *after* they are gone, or even when they choose to ignore it: 'Reality is that which,' said Philip K. Dick, 'when you stop believing in it, doesn't go away.'[8] This 'Reality' is not, however, always comprehensible in terms of the symbolic order people establish through/as language. In order to make the truth meaningful, even for a temporary moment, in order to attribute meaning, value, bias or purpose to it, it is necessary to transform language *beyond* language for the same temporary moment, to create a trans-subjective common subject/object in the intersubjective space, which can only be understood as revolutionary practice.

'Life, the Universe and Everything'

What Douglas Adams, the author of the cult classic *The Hitchhiker's Guide to the Galaxy*, taught us was that when we attempt the futile task of seeking the truth about 'Life, the Universe and Everything' (which is also the title of the second book of that series), the only answer we can get is '42'. Moreover, when we get that answer, we will already have forgotten what the question was. Thus, we have to spend as much time looking for the question of the answer we receive. The secret of Life is '42'. Or, if you don't like it, it's everything we do in order to live, survive, and change our lives. The secret of the Universe is '42'. Or, if you don't like that either, it's everything we do to open up to the universe, discover, understand, and change it. And *this* is precisely the secret of 'Everything': the revolutionary human practice that changes, transforms everything.

So, if you are looking for secrets about 'Love, Sexuality and Life' in this book, the only answer I can give you is, 42. If Love, Sexuality and Life had one (or a common) secret, it would be that love is never only 'love as we know it'; sexuality was not always experienced as we experience it today, and life has never had an independent meaning on its own, other than the one(s) we assigned to it:

> What does it mean? Meaning. And so we enter the realm of semantics. One must tread carefully here! Consider: from earliest times man did little else but assign meanings—to the stones, the skulls, the sun, other people, and the meanings required that he create theories—life after death, totems, cults, all sorts of myths and legends, black bile and yellow bile, love of God and country, being and nothingness—and so it went, the meanings shaped and

---

[8] Philip K. Dick (1978). 'How to Build a Universe That Doesn't Fall Apart Two Days Later'; in *The Shifting Realities of Philip K. Dick: Selected Literary and Philosophical Writings;* Vintage Books.

regulated human life, became its substance, its frame and foundation—but also a fatal limitation and a trap.⁹

There is a history of love becoming the monogamous, heterosexual, erotic love we know nowadays. It has changed from something else to what it is today, so it will not have to remain as we now experience it. Likewise, sexuality is not what we think it is: when two unicellular creatures temporarily fused together and separated again, not for procreation but for rejuvenescence, it was also sexuality. Even today, when we consider the forms it takes, gay and straight, sadomasochistic and fetishist, polygamous and monogamous, it is doubtful that we are even talking about the same thing when we say 'sexuality'. Consequently, today we can only imagine the forms it might take tomorrow – expectantly, eagerly or with horror and revulsion.

These aphorisms (theses, essays, whichever way you like it) try to fulfil one of the preconditions for imagining how we can fall in love tomorrow, what sort of sexual life we can have, and what kind of life we can lead. This precondition is to assume that the forms of love, sexuality, and life that exist here and now, are *not* absolute, immutable, frozen in their tracks. To realise that what is now considered 'normal', ordinary and self-evident, what is now accepted without discussion, without critical scrutiny, what are not even considered 'problems', should be problematised at all costs. Well, you can always ask, 'What is the point of causing trouble, of "rocking the boat", as it were, when everything is going quite all right'? Really? Does all this really look 'all right' to you? What popular, mainstream forms of psychoanalysis, psychiatry and psychology, as well as a significant portion of 'experts' in these fields tell us, is nothing more than 'stop rocking the boat, stop making trouble, and return to normal'. In the *DSM V*, the diagnostic handbook of Clinical Psychologists and Psychiatrists, for instance, you will find a 'disorder' called ODD, Oppositional Defiant Disorder. In a nutshell, it is the refusal to bow down to authority (especially in children and adolescents), and doing this in an angry and 'defiant' manner. What is more distressing is that, there *actually* are some psychotherapists who take this quite seriously! Neuroscientist V. S. Ramachandran describes this 'disorder' as follows:

> And let's not forget another notable invention, "oppositional defiant disorder." This diagnosis is sometimes given to smart, spirited youngsters who dare to question the authority of older establishment figures, such as psychiatrists. (Believe it or not, this is a diagnosis for which a psychologist can actually bill the patient's insurance company.) The person who concocted this syndrome, whoever he or she is, is brilliant, for any attempt by

---

⁹ Lem, Stanislaw (1973). *Memoirs Found in a Bathtub*. Tr. Michael Kandel and Christine Rose. New York: Seabury Press, 188.

the patient to challenge or protest the diagnosis can itself be construed as evidence for its validity! Irrefutability is built into its very definition.[10]

What most of these therapists suggest to their patients, who, in the case of this so-called ODD, are mostly children, is 'adapt, accept, endure, be content, obey'. Moreover, these 'therapists' are even worse than the despotic master who used to say 'shut up, submit, obey,' because that master was willing for us to keep our voice down and to obey in practice even if we rebelled internally. The kind of slavery that these pseudo-therapists see fit for us does not end there: they want us *to believe*, give consent, accept *willingly*, and be accomplices in our own subordination. They want us to normalise, settle for the average, worship banality. Psychoanalysis, however, which is a radical method in the most literal sense of the word, does not engage in normalising us, but with problematising what is passed as 'normal'; with 'rocking the boat' and 'making trouble'. Not because it is devoted to chaos, commotion and brawl, but because it knows from everyday practice that all these efforts for 'normalisation' actually never work; that they never achieve permanent results, that the repressed *always* returns. All the efforts for adapting to the ordinary, surrendering to the average, kowtowing to the 'self-evident' and obeying to what seems to be eternal and inevitable, end up in the emergence, the next day if not tomorrow, of new pathologies: new neuroses, phobias, sexual hang-ups, affective 'disorders', and eventually, life-and-death problems, profound melancholy, causeless mourning and, sometimes, suicide.

Institutionalized psychiatry and the institutional/conservative psycho-therapeutic methods that either emulate or complement it, try to *normalise* us first, and then, when the repressed inevitably returns, they dump the problem on pharmacology, if, of course, they haven't already done so. The labours of psychoanalysis, however, will begin exactly at this point, that is, where conformist psychotherapy retreats to drugs. There are, of course, many situations where the 'talking cure', including psychoanalysis, will not suffice to relieve the pain of the moment, and a variety of methods from medication to psychosurgery can be useful or even unavoidable. Unfortunately, these methods usually cannot go beyond being by-products of the Procrustes method in the hands of commercialised psychotherapy, which endeavours to fit everyone to the same 'normal' bed by detruncating the longer ones and forcefully elongating the shorter.

Accepting the indisputability of the 'normal', the incontestability of the self-evident and the predominance of the average, as immutable and without alternative, leaves us in despair. The most obvious and immediate remedy of

---

[10] V. S. Ramachandran (2011). *The Tell-Tale Brain*, NY & London: W. W. Norton & Co., 25.

this despair is legal or illegal, chemical or psychical narcotics. Once you accept that *this* is the only world possible, *this* is the only love that can be experienced, and *this* is the only form sexual relationship can possibly take, your destiny is either melancholy or murder, either never-ending boredom or insanity, either a dull success story or a series of defeats, either SSRIs or heroin. It doesn't seem to matter. Or maybe it does: If you really believe that *this* life, *this* love and *this* sexuality are immutable, eternal and absolute, my humble advice is to choose the former options, because where there is life, there is also hope; the latter options will either kill you or put you out of commission as a self-conscious subject.

But let's put this assumption of immutability aside: Murderers, lunatics, tenacious losers or junkies are not very different people from us. It is precisely for this reason that we strive to domesticate them, calling them 'victims of fate', 'mentally ill', 'losers' or 'substance abusers': when we look at them, we see ourselves, or at least an aspect of our selves, of what we might have been or what we may yet become. And not without reason: we are all victims of the same despair after all, hence our affinity.

The hope that another love, another sexuality, another life can exist could heal all of us. Like every 'cure', however, there is a price to pay in this option as well: In order to embark upon this journey, we have to engage in the ruthless criticism of *this* love, *this* sexuality and *this* life; we have to problematize them, to take them to pieces in our minds and then reconstruct them again. While we are at it, however, we will 'deconstruct' a lot of things that seem very dear to us now; we will be clumsy, we will be mean, and we will suffer and lose a lot in the process, *before* we are assured of success (if we wait for assurance first, the promised change will never come).

We cannot imagine tomorrow without the ruthless criticism of the present, and discovering in it what does not exactly belong in today, what is transgressive, revolutionary, belonging to tomorrow, but *real*. The mistake of the utopians from Plato to H. G. Wells, was that they tried to put the present aside and tried to imagine tomorrow as a fiction that would emerge only from their minds, starting from scratch.

We cannot imagine tomorrow without the ruthless criticism of the present, and discovering in it what does not exactly belong in today, what is transgressive, revolutionary, belonging to tomorrow, but *real*. The mistake of the dystopians from H. G. Wells to Orwell, was that they forewent grasping what is transgressive, revolutionary and belonging to tomorrow within today, and tried to imagine tomorrow as a much darker and exaggerated version of today.

We can engage in the ruthless criticism of today and start to imagine tomorrow. The point, however, is never to forget that we are a part of *this* today, the not-anymore, and *that* tomorrow, the not-yet.

CHAPTER 1

SOMETHING IS MISSING

> 'Have some wine,' the March Hare said in an encouraging tone.
> Alice looked all round the table, but there was nothing on it but tea.
> 'I don't see any wine,' she remarked.
> 'There isn't any,' said the March Hare.
> 'Then it wasn't very civil of you to offer it,' said Alice angrily.
>
> Lewis Carroll, *Alice's Adventures in Wonderland*

I. 'Something is missing' in our lives, in our every relationship. Heavens forbid, what if it weren't? How could we ever get rid of that relationship? A life in which nothing was missing would have been like heaven, or utopia. 'The difference between utopia and a cemetery,' suggests Ralf Dahrendorf, 'is that occasionally some things do happen in utopia.' (Dahrendorf 1971, 106)

II. In his 1971 film *Bananas*, Woody Allen tells us of the tragicomic relationship between New York Jewish intellectual, Fielding Mellish (Woody Allen) and New York leftist activist, Nancy (Louise Lasser). Every time right after sex, Nancy lights her cigarette or rolls her joint, staring at the ceiling. 'Something is missing,' he replies to Fielding's persistent inquiries. 'I don't know what happened, but it's missing.' After Fielding is dumped (inevitable, right?) he travels to San Marcos and becomes involved in the revolutionary movement there. Oddly enough –actually by some weird accident– revolutionaries are victorious and seize power. Fielding eventually returns to the US to find funding for the new regime, but wears a huge Castro-style beard to avoid recognition. They 'meet' again with Nancy. Unavoidably, they end up in bed. 'I have to confess something,' says Fielding, removing his fake beard after sex. 'I *knew* something was missing,' cries Nancy.

III. What is this mysterious something that is missing? According to the website, 'Sex as Nature Intended it' (http://www.sexasnatureintendedit.com), it is the foreskin. This site, which claims that circumcised penises are useless, that the highest sexual pleasure (for women) comes from uncircumcised penises, and even encourages women to urge their circumcised partners to have their foreskin reattached by surgery, tells us that it is the foreskin that seems missing to Nancy; Fielding –actually Woody Allen– is Jewish, after all.

IV. Being biologically male, culturally circumcised and preferentially heterosexual, it is impossible for me to know whether there really is a difference. But the website 'Sex as Nature Intended it' seems to have a valid point, albeit unknowingly, but in reverse.

V. It is true that what Nancy misses has some relation to the *phallus*. But is it possible to establish the same relationship with the biological genitalia, the *penis*? Doesn't seem likely. Even if Fielding Mellish/Woody Allen was uncircumcised, something would probably still be missing. Because a *lack* is not something that was lost, cut, ripped off. It is something that was never there in the first place.

VI. When we reduce the problem to the foreskin, we feel a little relieved. It was taken away from us against our will, without our consent. Moreover, 'Sex as Nature Intended it' website also tells us how to get back what was lost— for a small fee, of course. It's a minor, non-invasive surgery after all, like having a hymen re-stitched. When it's done, it will be like good as new, complete.

VII. The thought, on the other hand, that what was missing has never been there at all, scares us out of our minds. It's like a basketball match; we start forty points behind. Moreover –horror of horrors– it may not be missing in others. Well, on this point, at least, I can give some assurance: there is no such possibility!

VIII. What is missing then? We started with *Bananas*, let's stick with it: What could be lacking in those diminutive, usually Jewish, intellectual (or rather, semi-intellectual) New Yorker types, almost always portrayed by Woody Allen himself in many of his earlier films, who incessantly speak a lot, are often in a panic, suffer from acute anxiety and cannot be accused of being handsome or pretty by anyone? Can it be self-confidence?

IX. But what is there to be confident of? The man is more of a know-all than wise or knowledgeable. He is small and (let's be generous) not very handsome. He does not have any athletic abilities either; as in *Annie Hall*, he is pathetically clumsy even when he plays a friendly game of tennis. How do we expect him to be self-confident?

X. But on the other hand, even a know-all can act wisely from time to time. Is it necessary to be tall and handsome/beautiful to be charming? Woody Allen and James Cagney are the same height after all. Who can accuse John Malkovich of extreme handsomeness?

Something is Missing

Even if we are terrible athletes, we can enjoy the game if we do not panic, if we are not obsessed with 'winning', or looking ritzy all the time. The person who enjoys the game already looks pleasing to the eye—but not the other way around. A little self-confidence is enough for all this.

XI. And so we found our paradox: Unless I have confidence in myself, I will be an awkward, unattractive and clumsy know-all. How can I be self-confident when I already feel that I am an awkward, unattractive and clumsy smart aleck?

XII. When did we start feeling un-self-confident? When did we first become know-alls (or ignoramuses), unattractive, clumsy, incompetent? Or are we really like that? Do we feel that way because someone tells us that 'Something is missing,' or is it because we already feel something is missing that others tell us exactly what we expect to hear?

XIII. The lack has always been there. We have never been complete. We were lacking from the moment we were born, because the body with which we were one was taken away from us. From the moment we started seeing and knowing the world and establishing a 'self' of our own, we have always tried to cope with this deficiency. We could never entirely come to grips with being a separate, independent being, but had no other way to survive.

XIV. But isn't this Macbeth's curse anyway: 'None of woman born' can kill Macbeth? Macduff, however, is not 'born of woman', but was 'from his mother's womb / Untimely ripped,' (*Macbeth* V:7), that is, born by C-section. That's the reason he can bypass the curse and manage to kill Macbeth. This, in fact, is a somewhat feeble trick: a C-section *is* also a birth, Macduff *was* actually born of a woman. But the inadequacy of the device does not overshadow Shakespeare's genius: it is only the one that is not 'incomplete', not 'born of woman' (that is, taken away from another body) that will overthrow the sovereignty of violence. This is the reason we haven't been able do anything against the dominion of violence for millennia: there are, unfortunately, no such people.

XV. Or perhaps it is precisely the 'lacking' ones, those who have accepted and came to terms with this lack, who will overthrow the dominion of violence. In the third book of *The Lord of the Rings*, *The Return of the King*, during the Battle of the Pelennor Fields, the Lord of the Nazgûl cries, 'No living man may hinder me!' Tolkien's answer to the male-centred structure of the English language, which does not regard women as human beings but identifies humanity with masculinity, is simply this: 'But no living man am I! You look upon a woman. Éowyn I am…' With these words, Éowyn raises her sword and finishes off the Lord of the Nazgûl. The 'lack', therefore, can sometimes be 'an excess', and advantage.

XVI. We are born lacking, but we cannot name this lack. Then, if we are female, somebody tells us what we are missing is a tiny piece of flesh that is supposed be between our legs; not just the tip, as the 'Sex as Nature Intended it' website thinks, but all of it. Even if they don't say it, they will intimate, hint and imply. If we believe them and do not question this presumption, the rest of our lives will be spent trying to compensate for this 'shortcoming': by 'borrowing' it from a man, giving birth to a child (preferably a boy), or several/many children, or, on a more symbolic level, trying to emulate male behavioural patterns, attire, social status. Unfortunately, it's all temporary: sexual intercourse lends us the penis for a very short time; the child will be born and be separated from us (the counterpart of our initial break), and eventually leave us entirely; the status, the attire and the behavioural patterns we adopt are also temporary, and when push comes to shove, there will always be someone, some institution or some law/custom/tradition who will cruelly remind us of our most basic 'lack'.

XVII. But those of us who do have that piece of flesh should not be too self-confident either. They may have penises, but a penis is not enough to make up for the lack; far from it. Nothing that is promised to those with penises ('women', power, status, security, integrity, inclusion) is given to children. So we duly wait for the days we are 'grown-ups', for the time when all the promises will be kept.

XVIII. Some of us, those who are, let's say, more naïve, can mistake the metaphor for literal meaning, and assume that 'growth' is in the size of the penis. Men's magazines are full of letters from readers, whining 'My penis is not big enough!' Many men flock to psychotherapists (and/or other kinds of therapists) with the same complaint. News of penis enlargement treatments (chemical, surgical, mechanical) take up a considerable space on the internet, and our spam folders constantly overflow with hundreds of emails from unknown sources, promising diverse methods to increase the size of the penis (no matter whether we *have* one or not). We are consistently nudged, lured and bullied into 'Enlarging it!'

XIX. Even if we do not make this mistake, the eagerly awaited day never comes. Because the woman that we thought the presence of the penis promised us, is nobody but our mother; she was our first and only object of desire at the time we heard the siren call. Now that we have grown up, we have also learned that she is strictly forbidden to us; there is something called 'incest' after all. We will never become bourgeois or aristocrats or CEO's or world leaders overnight, just because we have penises (half of the world's population do anyway). It will not change the colour of our skin from yellow or brown or black to white. It will not magically transport us from a war-zone, a land of famine or a country under authoritarian/totalitarian dictatorship to a presumably 'democratic' and wealthy land.

XX. Because, unfortunately, the key that will supposedly open the door to power, that will fit in the lock, is not the penis, which is just another (and quite insignificant) body part at the end of the day. It is its Greek namesake, *the phallus*. The phallus is a sign that is visually based on the penis, but has become detached from it in the course of development of language to indicate power. But again, to our chagrin, we don't possess that either. Actually, nobody has it. Some just pretend they do.

XXI. The phallus itself is a sign of a lack. It's a sign of something we never have. Sometimes we just pretend that we had that something (although we can never precisely name it or say *when* we had it) and then lost it along the way. It doesn't matter whether we are a man or a woman: in both cases the phallus always points to a lack. Since men have an organ that biologically resembles a phallus, it is easier for them to cultivate the illusion of having had it but lost it somewhere along the way.

XXII. The phallus is a sign: the truncheon in the hand of the policeman, the slap of the father, the weapons of mass destruction. None of these makes up for the lack in their owner: neither the policeman nor the father nor the President of the USA have the power they believe that was promised to them. This is why they are incredibly insecure and therefore dangerous. With the intolerable awareness of having a lack, they can use the objects they have in hand, the surrogates of the phallus, in exceedingly irrational ways. The policeman torturing the prisoner, even though he does not need to learn anything, the father smacking the child for no reason at all, the USA using deadly force all over the world and almost always fumbling it: they are only trying to make up for that lack they are painfully aware of. Let's not be hasty, however, to be too understanding to the policeman who tortures to prevent a possible crime, to the father who beats his children to 'discipline' them, or to the USA, struggling to 'export democracy'. When these 'rational' explanations on the surface are scratched by the rain and the wind in a few days, or at most within a few years, what remains will be the same: torture, domestic violence, war.

XXIII. What all these people are really lacking is self-confidence, nothing else. The policeman thinks he is no good without his nightstick and his gun. The father got a scolding from his boss at his job; he was pushed by some bully on the street and was too scared to respond. The (thankfully, ex-) President of the USA cannot deal with his umbrella while entering a plane and cannot even walk straight down a slight slope. Which one of these is more self-confident than Woody Allen's characters, apart from bursts of arrogance which we usually mistake for self-esteem?

XXIV. Thus we complete the full circle and fall prey to the same paradox. But maybe we can find a clue, a hint of a solution at this point. The reason we perceive the situation as a paradox is because we mistake a lack for a loss, for something we once had but taken away from us.

XXV. The absence of something we have never had, something we do not even know what it is like having, gives us an uncanny feeling. It is not there, but what if it were? Would I have been more beautiful? Would I have been smarter, wiser, more attractive? Or would I have been entirely someone else, *something* else I didn't know, I couldn't even recognise?

XXVI. So, with a little sleight of hand, we cast a veil over the knowledge that what we lack was never there at all, and turn it into a loss; into something that we once had and taken from our hands, stolen.

XXVII. Well, since we did not accidentally mislay it (how could we mislay something *that* important?), somebody definitely stole it from us, torn it away from us, severed, snatched. The rest automatically follows: we invent someone, an *object*, who is supposed to have stolen what we lack, blame everything on them, and spend the rest of our lives directing all our resentment, hatred, anger and fury towards them. These could be Jews, Muslims, Blacks, 'intellectuals', communists, liberals, radicals, anarchists, atheists; anybody but us.

XXVIII. They become the robbers of our joy overnight. People who know something we do not, who have access to the secrets of our lives behind our backs. Those of us who are furious at the women in *hijab* are actually wondering what kind of satisfaction that is denied to us lies behind this attire. There must be, since they are dressed like this in the middle of the summer and not even complaining! Surely what was stolen from me is there. All black men have huge penises. Everybody says so, therefore it must be true. The villains! Down with them! These intellectuals are useless rascals, they know nothing but talk, talk, talk. But is it possible that among all that gibberish they possess the knowledge of something that I don't? A secret withheld from me? Devil take them!

XXIX. Do we feel a little better? No, we just managed to be a little (more) racist, a little (more) bigoted, a little (more) anti-intellectual, a little (more) intolerant. Good night, and good luck!

XXX. Going back to where we started: when Nancy said 'Something is missing!' after every time they had sex, which or whose 'lack' was she talking about? Judging by the course of events, Fielding's. We were already willing to believe it, based on Woody Allen's stereotyping. If there is something missing, we should seek for it in the insecure, clumsy, unpleasant, incompetent man.

XXXI. I have just suggested, however, that the lack is always in ourselves. We only project it onto someone else; onto an 'other'. There may be two explanations for the feeling of 'lack' in Nancy, one quite obvious and the other slightly more complicated. Let's postpone the complex one for later. The obvious possibility is that Nancy didn't/couldn't have an orgasm. That could be what was missing.

XXXII. There are usually several reasons for this. Let us not spend much time on anorgasmia: Of course, anorgasmia itself is not a simple problem, either, that can be explained away by physiological reasons and be dealt with in an instant by behavioural therapy, but let it stand for now. Nancy probably cannot have an orgasm because she cannot feel completely 'there' during sexual intercourse with Fielding. Her mind or soul or whatever, is elsewhere, and this elsewhere doesn't have to be another person at all.

XXXIII. Could this be due to a lack in Fielding, his indifference or 'poor performance'? One possibility is that the he is so focused on his own experience and pleasure that he is not even aware of the woman next to him, not realising what she is feeling or undergoing. This, however, is not very likely. The film was made in 1971. Although Shere Hite's *Report on Female Sexuality* (1976) had not yet been published, Kinsey (1953) and Masters & Johnson (1966) reports were there for years. It is almost impossible for a New York (semi-)intellectual to be unaware of these, and remain indifferent to a sexual/cultural environment in which female orgasm is constantly problematised and politicised. It is highly unlikely that a rather narcissistic person like Woody Allen, and the film character(s) he builds around his own personality, did not turn this into a performance issue, a question of accomplishment, a 'problem' to be solved.

XXXIV. This time, however, we will encounter another 'catch' and another problem will emerge; something we can call 'excess effort':

> Goodnight, my darling, I hope you're satisfied,
> The bed is kind of narrow, but my arms are open wide.
> And here's a man still working for your smile.
>
> Leonard Cohen, *I Tried to Leave You*, 1974

This is a song also from the '70s, an ironic expression of what can be called 'considerate male syndrome' of the intellectual who does his best to make his woman 'smile'.

XXXV. The 'selfless' and horrified (semi-)intellectual learns from the Kinsey and Masters & Johnson reports that the majority of women (a vast majority) do not have orgasms. In a state of panic, he feels the responsibility of his whole gender upon his shoulders, and desperately tries to 'orgasm' the woman lying next to him (consequently, of course, making it harder for her). This syndrome, of course, is not only due to a guilty conscience or simple good will: if the majority of women cannot reach orgasm, the reason must be the irresponsible and stupid men they're with. *I*, however, am different. There are two problems with this reasoning: First, it provides a narcissistic satisfaction by positioning ourselves on a higher level from 'other men', and secondly, it assumes that women's problems can only be results of men's actions. So, if the woman can have an orgasm, this is due to the man's success, if not, it is the man's failure. As it immediately becomes apparent, the women in this equation are again crossed out.

XXXVI. In this case, it is possible to talk about an excess, a surplus of effort and performance, rather than a lack. It is such an 'excess', however, which further emphasizes the flaw. A surplus that interferes with, intrudes in and cancels a woman's relationship with her body.

XXXVII. The lack, therefore, is in Nancy; not her *fault*, but it nevertheless is in her. Wasn't one of the liberationist slogans of the second-generation feminists of the 1970s, 'I am responsible for my orgasm'? Nancy does not take the responsibility; she leaves something missing, because she believes 'something is missing' already. Or maybe she is trying to tell Fielding something by leaving his excess effort and forced performance without a reward. What exactly is she trying to say?

XXXVIII. Now we can see that this 'simple' explanation actually depends on the more complex explanation we have postponed. Can Nancy actually be trying to tell Fielding, 'You are not "the One"'? Surely, we can ask her, if Fielding is not 'the One', why are you trying it with him over and over again? Wasn't insanity doing the same thing over and over and expecting a different result, in that famous catchphrase usually misattributed to Albert Einstein? And, by the way, who is 'the One' anyway? Is there really such a person? Can they be defined or described?

XXXIX. The search for 'the One' may indicate a lack in what you do have, but it may also indicate an excessive expectation, or an *expectation of excess*. Indeed, the second part of *Bananas* is the story of Fielding searching and 'finding' this 'excess', and *almost* fooling Nancy with it.

XL. But what is this 'excess' that Fielding discovered? Can it be the huge phoney beard he wears? The beard has a double meaning: First, it is an apparent reference to Fidel Castro, and as such, it points to an imaginary change in Fielding. The year is 1971. Castro is still a hero for the 1968 generation, not yet succumbed to the coming conservative wave. In an ideological sense, therefore, the Castro beard represents Fielding's turn to 'revolutionary' politics, and his transformation from being a cynical, sluggard, allegedly impartial intellectual who does nothing but talk a lot, through a *passage à l'acte*, into an actual agent.

XLI. But we know that this, too, is a huge lie. Both the movie *Bananas*, and the story it is based on, Woody Allen's 'Viva Vargas', tell us that the revolution in the fictitious country of San Marcos is in fact *anything but*; that the only reason for the victory of the revolutionaries is nothing but the dictator's and the government forces' utter stupidity and cowardice. The 'revolutionaries' neither have a plan or program for the aftermath of the revolution, nor do they have any hope that the revolution can actually succeed. As a matter of fact, in the original story 'Viva Vargas', power is seized 'accidentally' when the guerrillas march to the capital to surrender, only to find that the capital is accidentally bombed by the government's own air force and left wide open.

XLII. The supposed 'transformation' in Fielding, therefore, is actually as fake as a phoney beard. Nancy, however, *almost* swallowed this change, if Fielding (maybe due to his Jewish excess-conscience, his constant feeling of guilt) had not taken off his beard and 'confessed'. Even though Fielding seems to be changing, he's just as insistent on remaining himself.

XLIII. We can safely assume, therefore, that Nancy's expectation of a revolutionary, activist, self-confident man is as phoney as Fielding's fake beard and 'change'. The expectation expressed in those big words can easily fall victim to a fake beard. In short, we are dealing with a couple deserving each other.

XLIV. As for the second and pretty pedestrian metaphor, we can deduce from the shape of the beard that it is apparently a symbol for an 'enlarged' penis (or, more precisely, both the penis and the phallus). We can then imagine that Nancy's 'Something is (still) missing' complaint was in a sense also directed at Fielding's small penis; that the exaggerated beard promised a bigger one but failed to deliver.

XLV. What happened when Fielding put on a beard? Did his penis grow in size? No, but his phallus (the symbol of dominance, confidence, power) did, and that was enough for Nancy, who was usually content with symbols. Until, of course, the beard itself turned out to be phoney.

XLVI. 'I knew something was missing!' Of course she knew, how could she not? Because the lack can be corrected neither by a beard nor by a momentary *passage à l'acte*; neither by a seemingly radical change in political attitude, nor by a huge penis.

XLVII. The lack is always there, in all of us, at every moment of our lives. We live by trying to fill the gap, the fissure that the lack has opened in our psyche. Sometimes by holding someone else responsible for it, sometimes by trying to fill it up with another 'excess'. We fail, of course, but it is all for the better: that way we manage to relate to others, establish connections, relationships. Why would we need others if there was nothing missing? What if, reversing John Donne's famous poem, '[Each] man [were] an Iland, intire of itselfe?' Then we wouldn't be a 'peece of the Continent, a part of the maine.' Fortunately we are not islands. We are social beings thanks to our deficiencies and our lacks; thanks to *what is missing*. Knowing this, on the other hand, will not stop the lack from causing us constant anxiety and pain.

XLVIII. What is missing cannot be replaced, concealed, or even disguised. The art is in learning to live with it.

CHAPTER 2

KNIGHT IN SHINING ARMOUR

> You say you're lookin' for someone
> Who's never weak but always strong
> To protect you and defend you
> Whether you are right or wrong
> Someone to open each and every door
> But it ain't me, babe
> No, no, no, it ain't me, babe
> It ain't me you're lookin' for, babe
>
> Bob Dylan, *It Ain't Me Babe*

I. A significant part of our lives is spent waiting for a knight in shining armour to save us from loneliness, boredom, our family, our job, wanton unhappiness, a relationship gone awry, etc. (tick one or more as appropriate). When we find them (or when they find us), we rest for a while, then we start waiting for another knight in shining armour to save us from the first one. We seem to need a lot of knights, don't we?

II. We also have another version of this phrase in Turkish: The Prince on a White Horse, which is surprisingly not culture-specific. We never had an abundance of kings and princes in Turkish culture. At best, we had the Sultan and his heir, the *Şehzade*. There could be no other princes, because since Mehmed II in the 15th century, heirs apparent had their brothers strangled at the first opportunity, lest there would be a contest over the throne, a disturbance in the *ordo sæcularum*. Eventually, we were left with only the present Sultan and his one surviving offspring.

III. Obviously, then, the Prince on a White Horse is not a modest phrase at all, especially in Eastern/Middle Eastern geography. Those who are waiting for the Prince on a White Horse probably imply, 'I am worthy only of the Sultan, no less will do.' Unfortunately, there is only one Sultan, so get in line! If you get very lucky, you will find a place in the *harem*, to become one of the hundreds of women there.

IV. Seriously, if the problem is not narcissism at large, then the geography in question must be different: that phrase should belong to mediaeval Western and Central Europe, where kings and princes are a dime a dozen. The expression, then, must have been derived from the European fairy tales that started going around in Turkey in the Republican era, although it is not exactly 'Knight in Shining Armour' but closer to 'Prince Charming' who awakens Sleeping Beauty, saves Snow White, climbs up Rapunzel's hair, or to the Frog Prince who miraculously becomes a man when kissed by a princess.

V. The critique of these Fairy Tales by the second-generation feminists since the 1960s should be evoked at this point: What happens when Sleeping Beauty wakes up, when Rapunzel is rescued from the tower, when Snow White is finally free of the cruel stepmother, or when the frog turns into a prince, that is, what happens after the fairy tale is over?

VI. The classic ending of the fairy tales is: 'And then they lived happily ever after.' Feminists started their questioning precisely at this point and forward: What kind of a happiness is this? Who is happy? What is this 'ever after'? Will the Prince embark on new rescue operations, while the 'already rescued' woman wait for him in his house (or castle)? In short, replacing the Knight with the 'Prince' does not get the job done, quite to the contrary, makes it even more complicated.

VII. But wait! Where do we get the idea that these knights in Western European tradition, regardless of the colour of their horses or the glitter of their armour, are saviours in the first place? Apparently from European medieval romances.

VIII. Indeed, *Don Quixote*, the greatest parody/novel of the eighteenth century (perhaps of all time), tells us the story of poor Don Quixote, who tries to be a gallant saviour, a 'knight in shining armour', alas, in vain. His helmet is made of cardboard, his armour rusted, and his 'war-horse' only an old nag. There are no noble women around to rescue, no 'damsels in distress', no monsters to defeat, no brave knights to duel. Everyday life in all its mediocrity mercilessly passes by. Don Quixote desperately tries to insert a magical, heroic, idealized nucleus into this everyday life; he tries to disturb this mediocrity with his fantasies, but to no avail: the only thing he can achieve is to get beaten dishonourably at the end of every story. Cervantes has ruthless fun with the tradition of medieval romances of the three or four centuries that preceded him. In doing so, he also inadvertently invents a brand-new literary genre, that is, the novel in the modern/modernist sense.

IX. The question we should be asking ourselves is, then, were these knights really saviours? We learn from the records of the 13th and 14th centuries that these petty nobles called 'knights', whose only job was to fight, usually terrorized and plundered the countryside in Western and Central Europe for decades, when they were not doing the same thing in the Middle East. This mob, practically an unemployed horde when there are no Crusades or other campaigns, no expeditions to the East, cannot hold any productive jobs—not only because they are totally unqualified, but also it is not 'befitting' their social status. They were especially famous for not only shaking down and extorting the countryside, but also raping any and all women whenever they can, so much so that a local bishop even had issued a special circular forbidding knights raping noble women. The emphasis is on 'noble' of course, which proves that the real concern was not the act of rape itself, but the purity (rather, *knowability*) of the next aristocratic generation.

X. All in all, your average 'knight' will be more like Ser Gregor Clegane (aka The Mountain) in *The Game of Thrones* (novel 1996, TV series 2011-2019), big, dirty, crude, cruel, a killer and a rapist, than the knights depicted in medieval romances, although these latter are supposed to be *mimetic* works of art (and therefore closer to actual historical facts), while the former is downright fantasy.

XI. How come, then, we also come across a concept in these same romances that is referred to as 'Courtly Love', closely related to these romanticised knights? 'Courtly Love' is described as a kind of love that is almost totally Platonic, that is, completely free from sexuality. The knight in the stories that depict 'Courtly Love' is willing to face certain death for the handkerchief of the 'Lady', but does not approach her physically or sexually even when he gets the opportunity; he is content with mere symbols and he is proud in his constant suffering and seeming celibacy.

XII. The Lady appears in these epic stories in her inaccessibility. As soon as she is 'accessed', everything will turn upside down, the foundations of the world order will be shaken. Lancelot, for instance, the valiant knight *par excellence* in the Arthurian saga, is in love with King Arthur's wife, Guinevere, but buries his love in his heart, duels and decimates everybody who dare to 'stain' his Queen's honour, *until* he and Guinevere fall prey to Satan's temptation and make love one night. Camelot, the Round Table, the order that Arthur meticulously built (which will represent the national unity of England for later generations), abruptly come to an end the moment these two have their adulterous moment of bliss. Catastrophe follows.

XIII. What, in the scenarios of 'Courtly Love' in general, is the part assigned to the Lady other than being an unattainable object of desire? What does *she* desire? Does anybody have an idea what the lady herself desires? Will it be enough for her if the knight wanders around on his horse, polishing his armour, embarking on adventures on her behalf, thrashing those who slight her honour, and occasionally uttering words that seem poetic and very profound, albeit usually banal and incomprehensible?

XIV. Perhaps at this point we should stop and consider the difference between the real knight (or at least the one historical records tell us) and the knight in the legend (that is, the one medieval romances tell us). The former is a petty nobleman without any discernible qualities or occupation, the vassal of a stronger and richer nobleman. All he knows is how to use the sword and the lance, and to ride a horse. He is probably quite ignorant and rude. The latter, on the other hand, is a born poet with a sorrowful past. He uses his weapons eloquently and gracefully; when he fights, he elegantly moves as if dancing in his shining armour and colourful tabard.

XV. This last part about elegance and gracefulness is especially fantastic, because if you once tried to put on that heavy, smelly, creaking full-plate armour, you would quickly discover that in this armour you could only be as graceful as a tortoise on a donkey's back. One of the greatest achievements of John Boorman's usually underrated masterpiece, *Excalibur* (1981) was to insistently demonstrate the extreme clumsiness of these knights donning full-plate armour instead of romanticising them.

XVI. Here is the knight we have been waiting for all our lives: a mixture of these two figures. It is a combination, because even though a part of us thinks that the knight in shining armour 'we've been waiting for' is the knight of legends and romances, another part of us is glumly aware that that knight has no reality, and what we get in the end is Ser Gregor Clegane.

XVII. How, one is bound to ask, did we manage to create a romantic, well-behaved, platonic, fantasy figure out of an uncultured, boorish mob whose only skill was to use weapons, and harassed, raped, beat and murdered anybody who stood on their way in and

XVIII. out of Europe (if we include the Crusades) until the 17th century. Isn't this a bit too much of an exaggeration in turning things inside out and upside down?

XVIII. This inexplicable contrast could also give us a clue for a rational explanation: there must be something in that first (real, historical) figure of the knight, that is extremely *attractive* for us despite all the negative aspects, something we avoid to name or pronounce, that we have created a fantasy figure to cover up all its other features.

XIX. The first of these attractive aspects is probably that the knight bears all the imaginable phallic symbols on his person: the sword, the lance, the crest on his helmet, the full-plate armour that turns his body into a monolithic phallic symbol. But the second feature that immediately follows is that the knight's body is devoid of detail: his full-plate armour hides all features of his body, including his face, except for the eyes. As a result, the knight forms a uniform whole without any details, and therefore no flaws (the defect is in the detail).

XX. Precisely for this reason, however, *vuslat* is not possible: the knight cannot reunite with the beloved; in order to do that, he would have to take off his armour and turn into an ordinary person. In Boorman's *Excalibur*, when Arthur's father Uther Pendragon makes love to Igraine (which actually is a scene of extremely aestheticised rape), disguised as her husband by a trick of Merlin, he does not (cannot) take off his armour lest he breaks the illusion. As result, throughout the whole lovemaking scene we have to listen to a persistent metallic squeak.

XXI. What we desire in the knight, then, is *invisibility*. This desire, however, does not have a specific moment of satisfaction. As long as invisibility is constant, it seems as though satisfaction is achieved. But every peek in the armour, every hint of the naked body hiding under the shiny metal, is enough to overturn the desire.

XXII. Italo Calvino's novella *Il Cavaliere Inesistente* (The Nonexistent Knight, 1959) tells us the story of a knight from the Charlemagne era, Agilulf, who is nothing but an empty full-plate armour. His devotion to his king makes him go on 'living', but there is nothing alive in the armour. He is courageous, he is loyal, he is patient, but he is not 'present'. And we know in our heart of hearts that the knights we eagerly wait for are like Agilulf. They have all exceptional human values; they are beautiful, they are handsome,

	they are loyal, they are good, they are nice, but they do not exist.
XXIII.	So, invisibility actually corresponds to an absence: We wait for and desire knights in shining armour only as long as they do not exist. When they appear before us as real persons, in flesh and blood, they become ordinary, flawed, incompetent, clumsy. As an image of fantasy, they are amazing, perfect, elegant, beautiful. In order to remain so, they must forgo existence.
XXIV.	What does this absence correspond to in our everyday lives? If we consider the effort we put into rendering this knight inexistent, the literary stratagems we employ, the tricks we pull to deceive everybody including ourselves, it must be something we frantically don't want to happen.
XXV.	When we consider the terms 'knight in shining armour' and 'courtly love' together, we can perhaps see what this undesirable something is: Wasn't it sexuality that was missing in 'courtly love'? One of the important characteristics of real, historical knights, of the actual people *inside* the armour, is that they are famous as rapists. In romantic knights, this feature is reversed and sexuality disappears completely. Could the reason why we keep waiting for that romantic knight be because we actually desire a 'courtly love', a love that does not involve sexuality?
XXVI.	The knight in his shining armour will recite us romantic poems and look at us in adoration with his sorrowful, puppy-dog eyes. As soon as the armour is off, however, he will turn into a rapist. This is why the knight must be like Agilulf, and that armour must be completely hollow.
XXVII.	At this point, it will be appropriate to open a parenthesis on gender: we always assume that it is the women who are waiting for knights in shining armour. As a matter of fact, what is meant by courtly love is the imaginary relationship between the *Lady*, the object of desire, and the *man* who tries all kinds of shrewd tricks *not* to attain that object, ever.
XXVIII.	Yet, the Lady does not have to be a woman. And there is no rule that the knight should be a man. Without a doubt, there *is* such an assumption in the historical and literary context, but when it ceases to be a metaphor and becomes something pertaining to our real lives, the roles can shift and be reversed. Have we not known inveterate bachelors, men, who spent their lives waiting for the princess 'in a shining armour'? Or women who enter their relationships like a saviour, who stand out in their protective,

inclusive, supportive aspects rather than sexuality? Maybe they are fewer in number, but they certainly do exist. Let us never forget that one of the most famous 'armoured' figures in history was a woman, Joan of Arc. In fact, wasn't it precisely her armour, that is, 'wearing a man's attire', that was one of the main pretexts used by the church to burn poor Joan?

XXIX. Once gender loses its importance in assigning roles, we can also get rid of the 'heterosexual matrix', in Judith Butler's words, that is, of the truism that assigns all sexual positions we come across according to a simple binary, a 'male/female' dichotomy. Who knows, maybe Lancelot's real great love was Arthur himself, but since this would be considered an abomination at that point in history, (perhaps an absolute version of 'courtly love' in its impossibility), he had to make do with a woman supposedly 'belonging' to him, Guinevere.

XXX. There were instances of this even before the age of the knights: Achilles is wrathful about the ownership of the captive woman Briseis, has a heated fight with his 'king', Agamemnon, and retreats to his tent (an act unbefitting a knight, but there were no 'knightly values' at the time of Achaeans in which Achilles belonged). He returns to the battlefield, although he knows it would mean his death, to avenge Patroclus, his lover, who fought Hector disguised as Achilles (donning his armour) and was killed. Can one imagine a greater love than the one between Achilles and Patroclus? Let us not be fooled by the film *Troy* (2004), made by homophobic Americans, who made Patroclus Achilles' 'cousin' with a sleight of hand!

XXXI. Since women can play the role of the 'knight' in shining armour, and men can perfectly play the role of the 'Lady' waiting for the knight, it seems that the 'rape' in question here cannot be anything but a metaphor as well. Could those of us who are not tired of playing this 'knight in shining armour' game be confusing pure, unadorned, and unsublimated sexuality with rape?

XXXII. As I will argue later in detail, 'there is no such thing as a sexual relationship'. Perhaps some of us sense this absence, the impossibility, and because we refuse to face it head-on, we try to postpone the moment of *vuslat*, that is, sexual intercourse, forever. We turn, for instance a hollow, metal armour into our object of desire. After all, there is no *subject* in that armour that will objectify us or rape us (which is another word for absolute objectification anyway). Harmless.

XXXIII. I suggested that, 'We turn a hollow, metal armour into our object of desire,' but this is not entirely correct. Actually, we do not sexually 'desire' that hollow armour. That armour and the knight in it, is someone we *imagine* desiring us, but will never reach us. It makes *us* an object of desire, but since the position of 'object of desire' is actually a hollow position (an 'empty signifier'), it does not actually objectify us. Thus, we make an omelette without breaking the eggs (one of the alchemist's ultimate dreams).

XXXIV. Thus, our two needs are satisfied at once: we are both desired, our existence is approved, but we do not have to 'give' anything in return.

XXXV. Because we know, possibly from our own experience, but also definitely from centuries of 'romance' literature, that once we 'give it' we will no longer be desired. Because desire only lasts until the illusion of being satisfied is evoked; it ends at that precise moment and turns to other objects that have not yet 'given'. Then we will have to look for someone else to desire us. Tough.

XXXVI. Tantalisation, therefore, 'tempting but not giving', is not as nasty a trick as one might first imagine. It is much more innocent than it seems *prima facie*, much purer. It is only the expression of the pursuit for something impossible: we will no longer be desired when we 'give'; hence, we should refrain from giving in: a desperate hope for desire to last forever.

XXXVII. Undoubtedly, then, all these are nothing more than a little show for the benefit of the onlookers. In the end, we don't lose anything, but we don't gain anything either. We do not give, but neither do we *get* anything. We make an omelette without breaking the eggs, but, unfortunately, it is not edible. When our only goal is to be desired and to keep it going on forever no matter what, our relationship with our bodies and with the pleasures of our bodies is compromised and goes to waste in the process.

XXXVIII. Moreover, there is no guarantee that this strategy will always, or even most of the time, be successful: there is always the possibility that the knight (that is, the real person we temporarily 'appointed' to that position) may declare, 'And your quaint honour turn to dust, / And into ashes all my lust;' ('To His Coy Mistress', Andrew Marvell) and leave. But then that person will not be the Knight in shining armour anymore. Not only that, *they will never have been*, as it turns out: so that we can justifiably declare that 'they were just like the others.'

XXXIX. We desire, we want to be desired. Both of these are our right: because only when both are possible can we be both subjects *and* objects, human beings in the true sense of the term.

XL. But on the other hand, we don't want to attain what we desire, and don't want to be conquered when we are desired. Because both conquests throw the subject's subjecthood and the object's objecthood into doubt. The man who fell in love with us and recited fiercely romantic poems on our behalf, may sit in front of the TV in his wrinkled pyjamas and expect service (and nothing but service) from us, let's say, after a year into marriage (*vuslat*). Or once we 'conquer' the person we desire, we may start to have 'unbearable headaches' whenever the allocated time slot to make love approaches. Then neither the subject nor the object remains. Because in both cases the 'other' (both the 'other' as the object of desire, and the 'Other' as the subject that desires us) was imaginary. Once they became real, that is, when they became stabilised in actual 'others', they lost their significance and value.

XLI. Because desire is not a tangible emotion directed towards a tangible object; *it only pretends to be so.*

XLII. And we spend our lives trying to camouflage this (actually quite obvious) game. We cannot *not* play it, but if we pretend it to be too real, at some point we will have to admit that it 'is'. So, it is best to stand midway and turn our life into an endless waiting room, have our bread buttered on both sides.

XLIII. We have our bread buttered on both sides, but in the end, it slips from our fingers and we remain hungry as before. Our destiny, then, is similar to that of medieval romances: we are painfully aware that these romances eventually turn into either immensely ridiculous satires or pure melodrama. Even when they are melodramas, the audience can barely contain their giggling.

XLIV. Is anyone else deceived by this interminable camouflage? No. But we get along swimmingly, thank you very much, since everyone else is playing the same shell game.

CHAPTER 3

JEALOUS OF YOU I AM

> When I left they were sleeping, I hope you run into them soon
> Don't turn on the lights, you can read their address by the moon
> And you won't make me jealous if I hear that they sweetened your night
> We weren't lovers like that and besides, it would still be alright
>
> Leonard Cohen, *Sisters of Mercy*

I. We all get jealous—all the time. If we weren't jealous, how would we know we *owned* something? Wouldn't a world without jealousy be a world nobody owned anything? Or at least a world where they thought themselves not in possession of anything? The difference between envy and jealousy is perhaps the difference between not possessing something and feeling angry about it, and *dreading* that you don't own it at all and feeling desperate about it.

II. We should start by pointing out a peculiarity of the term 'jealousy': you can't use it as a verb. 'Jealousy' is a state (of mind), it is not something you *do,* unlike 'envy', which is quite close to 'jealousy' in one sense, so much so that they are often confused. When you are 'envious' of somebody, however, you 'envy' them, whereas when you are 'jealous' of somebody, you don't *'jeal'* them; there is no such verb, no such word.

III. This grammatical peculiarity can be attributed to the structural difference of the concepts: envy is something between two people; you *envy* someone, or at most you envy one of their features, something they possess. Jealousy is, or at least is supposed to be, between *three* people, forming a triangular structure. You are jealous *of* someone, *from* (?) someone else. We can see that it is not exactly certain which preposition we should use. How do I construct a sentence if I am jealous of my partner from the attentions of another person? What if it is my partner who is interested in that person? I am still jealous, but are *of* and *from* still appropriate prepositions in this case? Can they be used for every situation involving jealousy? Jealousy is usually limited to describing the subject's state of mind, rather than the real-life triangle.

IV. An old but still popular Turkish song goes: 'If your hair touches your face, I am jealous of your skin.' Here, the triangle of jealousy is established thus: (1) Subject; (2) The beloved's hair; (3) The beloved's skin. The first element (I) is actively 'jealous'; the middle element is the one to be 'jealous *from*' (your hair); and the last element is what I am 'jealous *of*' (your skin).

V. Having established the triangle thus, we come to our next and much more serious problem: 'The beloved' enters the equation as two separate objects, as hair and skin. Although these two objects are parts of the same person, the same entity, they are treated as two separate entities. So, jealousy begins by *splitting* the loved one, dividing them (at least) into two, and in doing so, cancelling them out.

VI. One version of the chorus of the same song goes: 'I'm jealous of you, I'm jealous of you from myself'. Due to the inappropriate placement of the prepositions, it is not even possible to translate this faithfully. In any case, however, the line exposes the problem more clearly. The triangle has now become: (1) Jealous subject (I); (2) Object of jealousy (The beloved); (3) The other to be jealous *from* (Myself). It means that jealousy is not content to divide the object of jealousy into two; *the subject* is also split, divided into two, and likewise, cancelled out.

VII. As we can see, it is actually the *other* in both cases that is cancelled out of this equation. Jealousy, then, is a two-person disaster. Either the beloved is split into two, one being jealous *of* and the other being jealous *from*; or the jealous subject is likewise split, one being the jealous subject and the other being the third, the one that it is jealous *from*.

VIII. Adam Phillips said, 'Three makes a couple.' The act of jealousy excludes all actual third persons, does not let anyone into the two-person structure, and creates the third (which is the *sine qua non* of language) by splitting one of the parties.

IX. The fact that the couple consists of three people is because two people need a third eye, a third figure, against which (or in whose gaze) they can assert and test their 'coupleness'. When jealousy makes even that impossible, however, we find out that the couple is not ready for this test. More seriously, jealousy also makes language impossible, because language always needs three elements: for dialogue (two-words) to be possible, we need a third element to position this dialogue against, opposite or facing it. Even the dialogues taking place in the strict privacy of our homes assume a third element, an imaginary audience; the big Other to construct our utterances in compliance thereof; the eavesdropping neighbour (imaginary or real); the best friend to listen to a one-sided summary the next day; the children trying to sleep in their rooms; anyone.

X. Once the third element is out of the equation, dialogue also becomes meaningless, futile. People do not hear each other anymore, and the two split figures I have tried to establish above, merge into an amorphous one: this is the jealous subject; without a partner or an audience. A desolate figure who can only relate to a single burning, devastating emotion, jealousy.

XI. We can, then, put aside the myth that jealousy is a side-effect, a by-product, of love/affection or desire/passion, because there is nobody else on the playing field but ourselves.

XII. The fact that we can cancel out both the 'Beloved' or ourselves so easily, means we do not know how to give up our selves. We cannot suspend our ego enough to be able to love, and we do not dare set sail for the unknown and the dangerous enough to be able to desire. When we cannot love or desire, only jealousy remains.

XIII. At the outset we said that jealousy was a two-person disaster. A disaster between the jealous one and the one being jealous *of*, in which case the person being jealous *from* is dismissed. But now we see that the person being jealous *of* does not exist either, at least as a real, tangible person. They do not have a gaze or a voice; they are completely assimilated in (or within the imagination of) the jealous subject, who can exist without them, even better if these are absent. They exist only as *property*, and they are bound to remain that way.

XIV. Can we say, then, that jealousy is essentially a one-person tragedy, a pre-Aeschylean one, taking place only between the protagonist and the chorus, representing the (imaginary) community? A beloved to be jealous *of*, or an other to be jealous *from* are just excuses, pretexts for us to be able to experience that desolate, desperate one-person tragedy.

XV. What is this jealousy, then, which turns people into solitary, possessed, wrathful, pathetic, wretched, miserable souls, and even murderers? Where does it spring from? Does it have a cure?

XVI. Perhaps it would be best to start by answering this: what do we feel when we get jealous? Jealousy, yes, but what does it feel like, how do we define/describe the emotion itself?

XVII. On the one hand, jealousy implies an intense sadness; a profound anguish rather than a simple gloom. It does not, however, resemble sorrow, or grief of disappointment, either. There is meditation and contemplation in both sorrow and grief; the search for and the inability to find the lost object; the emptiness left by what was imagined to be there and was not; expectation and loss, acceptance and rebellion. These are all complex emotions; in them conscious and unconscious aspects are mixed, intertwined.

XVIII. There is, however, no conscious aspect to jealousy. Of course, if there is a promise that is not kept, a deception or a broken contract, then a sense of justice, ethical concerns and a feeling of rebellion are also involved in it. But let us stop and think for a moment: is the jealousy we feel for someone with no contract between us, maybe even someone who doesn't even know us fundamentally different from the jealousy we feel when our lover or our partner cheats on us? Is the jealousy we feel for our spouse's ex-spouses (i.e., before they entered into a contract with us), or the jealousy we feel for our ex-spouse's future spouses, (i.e., after the termination of the contract), fundamentally different? There is no breach of contract, no violation of an ethical imperative or deception in any of these cases. The pain we feel, however, changes little, if at all.

XIX. Likewise, if a close friend with whom we do not have anything like a sexual relationship suddenly starts to act distant and find themselves a new 'buddy', a new 'BFF', perhaps (only *perhaps*) the amount of pain we feel will be different, but the *quality* of the pain will stay the same. Furthermore, whether this friendship is between persons of the same sex or different sexes will not change the feeling a bit. Without a doubt, a mischievous psychoanalyst may try to discover some hidden, repressed clues of homosexuality in many 'bromances' and 'soromances', and in some cases, they may even be justified; but this does not change the basic structure of our argument. The presence of sexuality, which puts us in our most naked, most vulnerable state, will probably intensify our pain, but the pain itself dates back to a time much before we learned about and experienced sexuality.

XX. The pain and anguish of jealousy, actually lies somewhere *before* ethical or rational concerns enter the picture. It is rooted in the pain of a newborn that suffers, but does not have the language to explain what its problem is.

XXI. Another emotion intertwined in jealousy is anger. But again, a different kind of anger. It is not an ethical 'wrath against injustice' which, Brecht ruefully accepts, still '[…] hoarsens the voice'. (Brecht 1939, *An die Nachgeborenen*), not even the possessive anger of the child whose toy is taken away. On the contrary, it is a desperate, primitive anger born of realising for the first time that something we never had, is/was not there at all.

XXII. This is, again, an infantile anger: the helpless but uninhibited anger of a baby pulled away from the nipple without warning, or, worse, when they wake up and realize that their mother is not there. This anger is different from the possessive anger of the child whose *toy* is taken away, because the baby does not 'think' it possesses the breast or the mother, but only feels it is *one* with them. That is why when they are detached from them, they once again realise that they are utterly, irretrievably alone and they become desperately angry. The babies have not yet comprehended or admitted that there is something called the 'I', and they are 'it'.

XXIII. So, being jealous is actually going back to our infancy, when we could not talk, we could not explain or understand our problems. Falling back into the emotions of that time that cannot be named, comprehended or made sense of. Undoubtedly, this regression is a complete defeat: it is an admission that that limitless inclusion to which we are trying to return, the illusion of being in unconditional unity with our environment, can no longer be experienced even as an illusion. So, the only thing that remains is the anger of the baby when they experience that this emotion is just an illusion (for example, when they wake up and don't find their mother at their side). For this reason, jealousy often leads people to violence. Because in jealousy, there is nothing that can be resolved with or within the limits of language: the emotion itself is pre-linguistic, pre-semantic.

XXIV. Jealousy is the transference of the of the profound and extra-semantic pain of the passage from one to two, to the signifiable but still painful passage from two to three.

XXV. We all go through the transition from one to two, from the moment we are born until the first kernel of an 'I' is formed. We were one with our mother, but now we're separate, torn away. We did not fully understand the meaning of this at the moment we were born (there was no 'meaning' and no 'understanding' at that time), but slowly as we see and recognize our 'self', independent of our mother, when that huge 'I' gradually broke down and became 'me and mother'. This is literally the most painful process of our life; the process of getting acquainted with loneliness, realising that we are tiny and powerless *vis-à-vis* a huge and meaningless world.

XXVI. Still, there is a consolation: The Mother. Although we are no longer one, the mother is always with us. Or is she? Which mother can constantly be with her child 24/7? The poor woman has chores at home, maybe she has other children, she has friends, needs to rest, maybe she also works outside the home; Above all, she has a husband (at least in the majority of families they do).

XXVII. In short, the moment we find solace in the eternal/external presence of themother and endure the pain of becoming two from one, (a) third element(s) emerges. Most of these are abstract (work, occupation, television, friends, etc.), but the other children and the husband (siblings and the father from our perspective) are always there in a very tangible way.

XXVIII. In fact, the rest of our lives will be spent trying to recapture and recreate that brief period of time between the moment we realise that we are an 'I' and the moment we realise that the bilateral relationship we have with our mother is not unique, impenetrable and absolute.

XXIX. Close friends, brothers, sisters, 'best buds', 'soulmates', 'BFFs', lovers, husbands and wives, 'father-and-son/like-friends', 'mother-and-daughter/like-friends', 'tomboy and father', 'mama's boy and mother': These are all pale images and imitations of the mother-infant relationship we had in that brief period.

XXX. We will always try to establish bilateral relations throughout our lives. These bilateral relations must be closed to the outside. In order to make the relationship meaningful, unique and absolute, there must be a secret to keep, a body language that others cannot fathom, code-words, hush-hush conversations, a common language unique to us, common memories that others cannot share, even if they know about them. When any of these are disclosed to third parties, they suddenly become worthless and meaningless. They didn't have any true significance anyway, other than establishing and maintaining that closed dual structure.

XXXI. However, this dual structure that we will try to build over and over again is under constant threat of repeating the destiny of that first model, the archetype, the original form. What is that destiny? A third comes in and shatters the (presumed) unity.

XXXII. We were one with the world, with the universe, with our mother, until we became aware of our own body and our self. There was no outside. Everything was inside. Then we realized that we were separate from our mother. At that time, we formed a closed bilateral relationship with the mother (who for us still represented the world and the universe). This new equilibrium was more unstable, perhaps, but we could live happily ever after in this state. *Until* the mother betrayed us, established the same dual relationship with someone else, or revealed to us that she had already had such (a) relationship(s).

XXXIII. The mother's bilateral relationship(s) with other siblings are dreadful, but often tolerable since they do not exclude us entirely. These relationships may even be beneficial for us because over time; they can play an important role in our learning to share, companionship, fraternity/sorority and solidarity. Of course, I am not talking here of the truly 'horrible' mothers who make obvious, hierarchical preferences among their children, who literally exclude some of them.

XXXIV. The mother's relationship with *her husband* (the father), however, must necessarily exclude us. Firstly, because the relationship between two adults in terms of language and memories will unavoidably leave us out, because it belongs to a world in which we are not yet included. Second, and more importantly, because there is an aspect in this relationship that cannot contain us: that mysterious thing we will later call sexuality. This relationship (which is initially our *raison d'être*) is the mother's obvious betrayal of us; that she does not keep his promise (What promise? The poor woman never promised us anything of the sort!), that she deceives us with another person (her husband actually, but our infant mind cannot yet accept this bit of legitimacy).

XXXV. The anguish that we feel when we realize that we are not one with the universe, the world, the mother, and then partially soothed ourselves in a closed relationship with the mother, reappears with this 'betrayal'. Fortunately, we will also forget this second appearance completely in the future. Because in the future, they will teach us what is right and what is wrong, what is legitimate and what is illegitimate, what is fair and what is unfair, and, most importantly, who is the boss and who is subordinate to them. Then the rebellious wrath we felt at that moment will become 'wrong', illegitimate and unfair, and it will be completely meaningless because it is directed against the 'boss' (the adult man, the alpha male, our father). The best thing to do, then, is to forget that pain, that rebellion, that feeling of betrayal.

XXXVI. But unfortunately nothing is solved with a simple 'Forget it!'. The same feeling will rush back at the earliest opportunity to haunt us, when the first bilateral relationship we establish outside our immediate family circle is threatened by a third, no matter whether literally or completely in our imagination. It is this feeling we will call 'jealousy'.

XXXVII. At its core, jealousy is a very simple emotion. It is one of the most primitive feelings possible. Someone we connect with through a real or imaginary relationship, by contract, or by fantasy offers us an illusion of our most primitive state of being 'one'. If anything threatens this illusion of unity, we feel the most primitive, most basic pain and we are filled with the most primitive, wildest anger.

XXXVIII. For this very reason, jealousy can never be fully understood, justified or comprehended though reason. The man has the same feeling when his wife cheats on him, as when the girl with whom he was secretly in love from a distance flirted with someone else. The woman is as intensely jealous of her husband's ex-wife, as with his female colleague with whom he has no (sexual or emotional) relationship. Even if the husband has a temporary 'adventure', the feeling will not change.

XXXIX. The problem is that we constantly dread that the person whom we think constitutes a closed whole, an exclusionary 'unity' with us, will create another union that is closed *to us* with another person, excluding us. Even when this is not the case, we will constantly nurture the delusion that they will do so sometime; that that person will become *like our mother*. Then we will immediately regress to infancy, remember the (not necessarily merely sexual) relationship between our mother and father that excludes us, remember the 'betrayal' of the mother. In fact, we will not actually remember the event itself (if we did, the problem would have been solved), but the horror that the mother has already left us; the pain, the anger, the anguish caused by this desperate, destructive horror.

XL. But on the other hand, since it is the product of a regression to infancy, to a period where fantasy and reality, life and imagination, experience and fear cannot be distinguished from each other, whether that jealousy originates from fear, delusion or a real event will not make any difference in the intensity or the quality of the emotion itself. As a result, many, if not most, murders originating from jealousy are not caused by actual cases of unfaithfulness or deception, but rooted in speculation, suspicion and sheer delusion. Consider the number of self-righteous men who kill their ex-wives or ex-partners, before the poor women even had a chance to have a relationship with a new person.

XLI. The underlying event in jealousy is the first step towards the ultimate separation of the mother and child. It is the beginning of the process that leads from a private world of two to a world of three (and more) people, eventually to community and society. Therefore, it is inevitable.

XLII. In his 1960 film *Psycho*, Hitchcock tells us the drama of Norman Bates, who has failed to dissociate from his mother. Bates has lived in a closed, bilateral relationship with his mother until his thirties, running their small motel. There is no father, not even his *name*. This small world-for-two is forbidden to third parties, and consequently, Bates has had neither a friend nor a lover in his life. One day, when the mother expectably and inevitably betrays Norman and attempts to get into a relationship with another man, he does the only thing he can and kills her. But since he cannot separate from her, he treats her dead body as if alive and keeps it 'at home'. Now Norman has to live a life for two, both to cover up his murder, and because he can no longer return to a one-person existence. He will greet the women he meets at the motel reception as the quiet, humble, introverted Norman, and kill them as the jealous and vicious mother who will never let another woman enter his son's life.

XLIII. This is undoubtedly a case of psychosis. But isn't this one of the basic definitions of psychosis? The inability to separate with/dissociate from the mother, the inability to form an independent self with definite boundaries, a certain beginning and an end.

XLIV. If we accept to be a psychotic, we would have no problem with jealousy. In this case, there wouldn't be an 'other' to be jealous *of* or jealous *from*. But there wouldn't be an 'I' either.

XLV. It means, jealousy is one of the prices we pay to avoid this psychosis. This is why it looks very much like psychosis itself, like most cures which resemble the ailment. Perhaps it is a more limited, more controlled psychosis that is squeezed into a specific, narrow area of life, a *vaccine*. But given the primordial pain and anger it invokes, its tendency to return to a pre-linguistic infancy, its abandonment of reason, logic and ethics, albeit temporarily, it is definitely a psychotic symptom. Like the vaccine it resembles, however, it may sometimes get out of control and become as lethal as the sickness itself.

XLVI. Whether we like it or not, we surrender a part of our lives as hostage to jealousy, lest we lose all of it.

XLVII. We all get jealous—all the time. Because we fear and hate any relationship that excludes us. We want our every relationship to be exclusionary in one way or another. In every relationship we establish, no matter whether we are a woman or a man, we are jealous of our mother from our father.

XLVIII. We were betrayed once. We never understood the reason for this betrayal, nor the scope and extent of it. As a result we are sentenced to re-live it over and over again in every relationship we have, and call this mindless, desperate repetition, jealousy.

XLIX. Perhaps one possible solution is to crowd out this mother-father-child triangle by including siblings (genetic, social, or chosen). Without a doubt, we are also jealous of our brothers and sisters, and they are jealous of us as well. We constantly fight them, we will be immeasurably envious if we see something in their hands that we do not have. We rat on them, we denigrate them, trying to get in the good books of our mother or father. In short, all the evil and wickedness we will commit as adults, we first try them on our brothers and sisters.

L. We can, however, do something very important with them that we *cannot* do with our mothers or fathers: solidarity, cooperation, complicity. When we try to do these things with our parents, they only metamorphosise into compliance, subservience and obedience. Except for some special cases where the age difference is very great (Freud himself comes to mind), our siblings are our *peers*. This is why the relationships we have established with them do not have to be faint replicas of the relationship we have with our parents.

LI. If we can manage to achieve meaningful relationships with our (genetic, social, or chosen) siblings that at least push the boundaries of the mother-father-child vicious triangle, then perhaps we can begin to imagine a life of less jealousy, more sharing and more solidarity.

LII. Jealousy is a mourning for a paradise lost; a lament for a utopia unachieved. If we can give up our desperate and impossible longing for perfection, we can have, as Berdyaev would have called it, '*une [vie] non utopique, moins "parfaite" et plus libre.*'

CHAPTER 4

THAT DARK/OBSCURE OBJECT OF DESIRE

> Ah! *Vanitas Vanitatum!* which of us is happy in this world?
> Which of us has his desire? or, having it, is satisfied? — come, children, let us shut up the box and the puppets, for our play is played out.
>
> William Makepeace Thackeray. *Vanity Fair*

I. Some of us, most of us, at times all of us, show an incredible insistence on desiring the worst for ourselves. As if there were some benefit in harming ourselves. Do you think there is some truth to this? Is there really any benefit that we can derive from self-harm? If not, how else could we explain this insistence? Is it sheer stupidity? For some reason it seems easier for some of us (most of us, at times all of us) to admit stupidity than to ask some dangerous questions.

II. In Alfred Hitchcock's *Suspicion* (1941), Lina (Joan Fontaine) marries the gambler, liar, scammer Johnnie (Cary Grant), rather than Reggie, her decent, honest, responsible childhood friend who is madly in love with her. As a result of this choice, the poor woman's life is wasted in 'suspicion'. Does the man she married really love her? Is he lying to her; if so when and how? Is he really a murderer? Or is he planning to kill him for her inheritance? The woman who pursues her desire in the choice between decent and peaceful dullness and dark fascination will never find peace again.

III. Men, however, should not think they are immune, either: In another Hitchcock film, *Vertigo* (1958), this time a man, Scottie (James Stewart), pursues his desire and falls in love with Madeleine (Kim Novak), a lying, slippery and mysterious woman evidently involved in something sinister, rather than the decent, supportive, affectionate but quite plain Midge (Barbara Bel Geddes) who is in love with him and offers a life of peace and quietude. In this instance, too, peace succumbs to desire and disappears, never to be found again.

IV. I am almost sure that most will agree with the heroes/heroines of these movies, without exception. Who would give Barbara Bel Geddes a chance when the alternative is Kim Novak?

Barbara Bel Geddes played Miss Ellie in *Dallas* in her old age, a pretty, clean-faced woman who could be anybody's elderly aunt or grandmother. She was not much different when she was young, either. Who cares whether Cary Grant is a liar or a gambler? Think about his devilish charm.

V. Can (at least a part of) the problem be our unwavering belief that charm and tranquillity are always on the opposite ends of the spectrum, as well as the equally strong conviction that our choice will always be on the side of trouble? Cary Grant is handsome, attractive. His character is a troublemaker. Well, couldn't it have been the other way around? For example, would Cary Grant be equally attractive to us if he played that decent and dull childhood friend? My guess is that he wouldn't have been. What appeals to us seems to be the promise of trouble itself, rather than good looks or beauty, or some undefinable 'charm'.

VI. The object of desire appears to be 'dark' in both examples. The name of Luis Buñuel's famous movie is *Cet obscur objet du désir* (That Dark/Obscure Object of Desire, 1977): I think the key word here is '*obscur*', which may mean 'dark' as well as 'ambiguous', 'vague' and, yes, 'obscure'.

VII. The object of desire is indeed *obscure* in Buñuel's film, because the leading role (Conchita) was played by two separate actors (Carole Bouquet and Ángela Molina). Moreover, since these women do not look alike at all, the audience is constantly confused throughout the movie, seeing one actor in one scene and the other in the one immediately following it; Bouquet walking into a room as Conchita but Molina coming out as the same person.

VIII. When you start looking for rhyme and reason in this fact, you immediately start inventing explanations, that, for instance, since one of the actors is a sensual and emotional Latin beauty and the other a cold, distant Anglo-Saxon (actually French) belle, this situation represents the two-facetedness of desire. The film is a story of tantalisation, of 'show but not give'; so, another explanation may be that Molina represents the 'showing' and Bouquet 'not giving'. Then, while we are swapping explanations and theories all around the place, Buñuel steps in and declares that it is merely a coincidence caused by one actor quitting the film in the middle of the production. The uncertainty is real; it is blind chance, bad luck; it resists, it denies your efforts to insert meaning in it.

IX. Without a doubt, Buñuel's declaration that it is sheer coincidence is not a statement that should be accepted unconditionally, at face value. First of all, he is playing with us, because after further investigation, we will find out that the actor that quit the film during production is neither Molina nor Bouquet, but *Maria Schneider*, who is not seen in the film at all. That is, she quit the film before the shooting begun, and it was not at all necessary to 'share' the character between two actors.

X. Furthermore, having the same role played by two separate and quite dissimilar-looking actors is not a choice lightly made. Indeed, at that time it was unprecedented in the history of cinema. Since then there are a few more examples, the most outstanding perhaps being Terry Gilliam's *The Imaginarium of Doctor Parnassus* 2009, but only after the leading actor, Heath Ledger died during production, and his role was 'shared' between three more actors in addition to keeping his scenes that were already shot.

XI. So, although Buñuel does not (or does not *seem to*; we can always expect mischievousness from him) attribute a specific meaning to it, he is still telling us that it is not important whether the object of desire which brought poor Mathieu (Fernando Rey) to his destruction is 'this' or 'that' Conchita. Those who already know Buñuel a little, at least those who have already seen *Belle de jour* (1967), will know that the object of desire is usually an ordinary *object* in his films: thus, the object of desire in *Cet obscure objet du désir* is the canvas sack carried around aimlessly throughout the film.

XII. That dark/obscure object of desire is not a woman, nor is it a man; it is just a crude, shapeless sack.

XIII. We always know 'something is missing' in our lives; The object of desire is that missing something. The problem is that we can never precisely identify what it is. The lack exists only as a lack, it will never be exactly defined, the void will never be filled, we will never be whole.

XIV. Those of us who are aware of this impossibility (like Buñuel) try to give others a message by making the object of desire invisible, uncertain, eventually completely shapeless. When we think that we are madly in love, when we are obsessed with someone, when we are desperately helpless in the face of an irresistible attraction, we actually assign a person to that position of the amorphous, shapeless object. The appointed person can be a woman, a man, gay (male or female), a trans person (male or female) or a bisexual; it doesn't matter.

XV. Let us create a list of possibilities, if you wish, by sampling the dynamics from films whose narratives are based on pure desire: In Buñuel's film *Cet obscur objet du désir*, the object of desire is a woman, but in fact, a woman who is played by two different actors whose physical and mental characteristics are fundamentally different. In Tennessee Williams' play *A Streetcar Named Desire* (1947; and in Elia Kazan's movie of the same name, 1951) it is a male. In Pedro Almodóvar's *Todo sobre mi madre* (All About My Mother, 1999) the object of desire becomes a trans person, Lola, whom everyone desires, regardless of gender, and who transmits HIV to everyone. In Pier Paolo Pasolini's *Teorema* (Theorem, 1968), the object is again a man, but everybody desires him, this time regardless of class *or* gender (servant, wealthy family members, women and men alike).

XVI. In *A Streetcar Named Desire* (or rather, in Elia Kazan's version), the object of desire is Stanley Kowalski, played by a young Marlon Brando in his hunkiest. He is rude, he is ignorant, he cannot even speak properly. But when he returns from bowling in his sweaty t-shirt, neither his wife Stella (Kim Hunter), whom he sometimes beats, nor his alcoholic sister-in-law Blanche (Vivien Leigh), who apparently believes that being a southern belle is a kind of nobility, can resist his animal magnetism. This irresistible attraction is not only because he is an object of desire in the general sense of the term, but also an object of *lust*. In Marlon Brando's persona, we see the purely sensual or bodily side of desire.

XVII. But even if everything begins with this sensuality, it doesn't end there: When Stella kicks Stanley out after a fight that again ends up in physical violence, the most famous (almost iconic) scene of the movie begins: Stanley is down on the street, yelling 'Stella! Stella!'; in this howl, however, there is neither anger, nor a hint of the violence we observed only minutes ago. Only a profound, deep-rooted, irreparable sense of loss; not even a loss, but a primordial lack, an utter deprivation. Having taken refuge in the neighbours' apartment upstairs, Stella is lured by this primitive, animalistic call and goes out, starts down the stairs, despite all the objections from her friends. The moment their eyes meet is like the definition of desire: it is so naked and intense that the scene becomes almost *pornographic*; that is, as in Žižek's definition of pornography, 'it reveals all there is to reveal' (Žižek, *Looking*

Awry, 1992); it does not leave anything hidden. This revelation of pure desire, however, will not prevent Stanley from beating Stella again in the future.

XVIII. I will not suggest, in a banal pseudo-psychoanalytic inversion, that what Stella really desired was a beating. No, Stella's real object of desire is that dark, obscure *thing* in Stanley. Those who snicker and read 'the thing' as a *penis* in a semi-slang shrewdness are not completely wrong, but they are not right either. That obscure *thing* in Stanley is so dark that it almost contains *both* the aggression/innocence of the 'Momma! Momma!' cry of the baby (it even regresses before that and becomes a howl without words and meaning), *and* the shamelessly self-confident, insolent male violence of the patriarchal order.

XIX. It is possible to see the same ambiguity in Almodóvar's Lola and Pasolini's anonymous 'Visitor': Lola, that woman on the outside and man on the inside (or man on the outside and woman on the inside, whichever way you prefer), that 'fatal attraction', has seduced everybody regardless of gender, and eventually infected many with HIV, which was still considered extremely deadly at the time the film was made. Throughout the film, the object of desire is only present as a name, as a myth, who constantly escapes our gaze, whom the narrative relates only sideways, almost never catches frontally until the very end. Once she is fixed by the camera, however, she loses her uncanniness and proves to be just another lost soul who is also dying of AIDS. As soon as we catch her, she immediately ceases to be an object of desire: a father disguised as a woman, a woman with the curse of '*le-nom-du-père*', a postman the letter she delivers was actually written to her, an aching void, a black hole that had tried to be both a man and a woman and failed to be either.

XX. Like Lola, the nameless Visitor in the Pasolini's *Teorema*, Terence Stamp is also a candidate to become a universal object of desire, with apparent religious connotations, but without a clear indication whether he is the devil or a saint. In the typically bourgeois family he invades, the father and the servant, the mother and the son alike are attracted to him. They all, however, move to another level of awareness through this attraction, rather than be destroyed. In his usual playfulness, Pasolini does not tell us whether this is Satanic temptation or spiritual enlightenment, although he does drop hints towards either direction. When the Visitor finally leaves (because the object of desire is unattainable, unretainable) everyone has come to a different place than they were in the beginning. We can never be sure whether it's for better or for worse, but they're not the same people anymore.

XXI. Buñuel had shown us the ambiguity and vagueness of the object of desire; pursuing that object was like a step into meaninglessness. In the Williams/Kazan example, however, the object of desire was strongly associated with lust and/or violence, from the infant's unreasonable, illogical and pre-semantic violence to the adult violence of the arrogant man, confident in the power of the phallus. In Almodóvar, desire went beyond violence and became lethal. Unlike all three, Pasolini is the only one who has managed to throw in a glimmer of hope in the obscurity and darkness of the object of desire. This hope does not necessarily have to be optimistic, but there is a guarantee: *Desire will change you for sure.*

XXII. Now we can return to the question we asked at the beginning: Why do some of us, most of us, at times all of us, show an incredible insistence on desiring the worst for ourselves? Because this is exactly what desire is: refusing to pretend that what the existing order offers us as reasonable, permissible and legitimate, and turning towards what is prohibited. And of course, when you turn towards the forbidden fruit, bad things will happen to you.

XXIII. Wasn't that exactly what Adam and Eve have done? If they had not eaten that forbidden fruit, they would have lived on in the Garden of Eden, not knowing pain, lack, and scarcity for ever and ever, but also without reproducing, not knowing bliss, sacrificing pleasure for peace, wonder for security, learning for a hollow, meaningless 'knowing' (*not* in the Biblical sense). How calm, how safe, how boring!

XXIV. It is one of the oldest myths of humanity: to turn towards the one forbidden object, while there are an unlimited number of reasonable, permissible and legitimate objects lying around, and to be handed eternal punishment as a result. Those who created this myth must have known something.

XXV. As a matter of fact, the only thing Adam and Eve learned when they ate that forbidden fruit was that they were naked. When they hide, shameful of their nakedness in God's gaze, they betray what they ate and learned as a result. Even God himself accepts that, by eating the forbidden fruit, 'The man has now become like one of us, knowing good and evil?' (*Genesis* 3:21) Since God could not have lied, it means that the knowledge of good and evil is indeed the knowledge of nakedness and shame, or, in short, sexuality.

XXVI. This is the two-sided, hypocritical, Janus-faced quality of desire: It means trying to peek in secret at what is forbidden and taboo, while pretending to seek pleasure and satisfaction. It constantly asks us whether there is something beyond what is this-worldly and human, and forces us or lures us to go and 'take an innocent look'. It doesn't help if I have thirty-nine keys. The object of my desire will always lie behind the fortieth door that is forbidden to me.

XXVII. This is precisely why Lacan tells us that desire seeks enjoyment (*jouissance*), rather than pleasure. Jouissance is not just pleasure; at its core it always contains something dark and malicious, something pertaining to death. That is why it is prohibited.

XXVIII. What is forbidden is not simply prohibited by the design of some evil forces to turn us into obedient slaves, at least not entirely, even though it is used to this effect most of the time. Behind every taboo, lies a flicker of truth distilled from thousands of years of human experience. Those who enforce these prohibitions *do* know something, if not as individuals, then as conveyors of a collective unconscious. The incest taboo, for instance, exists not only as a remnant of some random ancient tribal custom; it is there (no matter whether its enforcers are aware of it or not) to separate us from our mothers, to make us individuals with a sense of selfhood. Or, when our mothers yell 'Don't!', they are not haphazardly exerting authority; they are only trying to make sure we don't burn ourselves, or, worse, we don't get electrocuted.

XXIX. As a matter of fact, everybody knows something. This is why we keep chasing after the forbidden and the taboo: we desperately try with pathetic insistence to be one of the ones 'in the know'.

XXX. Remember what our first curiosities were? 'Where did I come from?' and 'What mischief are my parents concocting behind that closed door, hidden from me, excluding me?' We will get answers to both questions over time. Both answers, however, will be far from satisfactory. The answer to the former is that we break out from a space between our mother's legs, a space very close to where also urine and faeces come out. The answer to the latter is that they are threshing about after a very primitive pleasure, making bizarre sounds and doing weird acrobatics. In neither answer can we find even a trace of the transcendence we expect, the solution to our every problem, the balm to cure our each and every wound.

XXXI. By positing these two questions as *existential*, however, as existential as we can get as infants, we have already associated our most basic desire with them. So, throughout our lives, we will have to believe that 'that dark/obscure object of our desire' resides somewhere between reproduction and sexuality. It is also something 'dirty', since we will have also 'learned' through our toilet training that urine and faeces are filthy.

XXXII. Even if we say, 'But this is not it!' at the end of each attempt, we just can't stop trying. We unconsciously but firmly believe that somewhere between the 40th child and the 5,000th lovemaking, the secrets of the universe will be revealed to us.

XXXIII. For most of us, there is no time to achieve the 40th child or the 5,000th lovemaking anyway. Usually after the first try, we see that the information we are looking for is not there. Because when the object of desire ceases to be forbidden, it also ceases to be an object of desire. Didn't Buñuel's Conchita almost openly admit that she was not willing to achieve *vuslat* because she very well knew this? Conchita is reluctant to be Mathieu's wife, lover, or mistress, knowing that only the forbidden, the inaccessible will remain the object of desire. She knows that once she accepts one of these positions, Mathieu will sail away in pursuit of new objects of desire. Interesting woman, Buñuel's Conchita: she prefers being and staying the object of desire, a position which offers its resident absolutely nothing at all, over *both* lovemaking and sexual satisfaction, *and* marriage and social/economic security.

XXXIV. It is this quality that makes Conchita 'dark/obscure'. Acknowledging and embracing the meaning of being an object of desire, and carrying it to the extreme.

XXXV. One of the significant concepts in the *Torah* may clarify this issue: There is a verb in the Bible that is mentioned almost nine hundred times (873 times in the *King James Bible*, to be exact): the classical Hebrew word, *'yada"* (ירט'). This verb means both knowing and having sexual intercourse (hence the joke, 'Know, in the Biblical sense'). That is why we can come across this sentence in the *King James Bible*: 'And Adam knew Eve his wife; and she conceived, and bare Cain.' (*Genesis* 4:1) We have no doubt what it means, since Eve conceives Cain right after this act of '*knowing*'.

XXXVI. If knowing and having sexual intercourse are the same verb in classical Hebrew, one of the most ancient languages, we may need to take this matter a little more seriously.

XXXVII. We often do not think of desire in any sense beyond sexual desire, whereas desire is at the same time and always the desire *to know*. When Eve was first seduced by the Serpent and took a closer look at the forbidden fruit, she 'saw that the fruit of the tree was good for food and pleasing to the eye, and also desirable for gaining wisdom.' (*Genesis* 3:6) This is why the object of desire must always be dark and uncertain. Why should we desire something that stands in the light and is already known/defined? We already know it. In order to 'gain wisdom', we need to dare look into the unknown, into the dark, into the Abyss.

XXXVIII. I guess that's exactly the reason why we should stop constantly confusing desire and love. In order to love something, we need to *know* what it is. With desire, it is just the opposite. In order to desire, the object of desire must be dark, obscure, indeterminate; at least partially.

XXXIX. On the other hand, in order for us to continue to love, there must always remain something that is not yet known, left in the dark.

XL. Absolute acquaintedness is the feeling that there is nothing left to learn, the end of curiosity and wonder, it is the demise of love. In pitch darkness and the absolute absence of knowledge, however, love can never begin. There may be desire, but love does not arise from that desire; only a fatal, destructive passion/obsession.

XLI. If it is our greatest wish is to remain an object of desire, then we can reach and maintain this goal by sheltering and hiding ourselves, by not-giving, by burrowing behind a mystical veil and by lying constantly. But in the final account, nobody will have loved us in the true sense of the word.

XLII. If our one desperate need is to be loved, if we cannot do without being loved, it means that we will make ourselves transparent and expose our naked inner selves to the world. That way we can definitely be lovable and endearing, but then there will probably not be a soul who will desire us.

XLIII. The problem in both these cases is that we conceive of ourselves as *objects*: we want to be an object either of love or of desire.

XLIV. It should always be kept in mind, however, that there is also an option to be *subjects* who desire and love, preferably do both. When we are able do this, we may have a chance to become subjects who *know*, in both senses of the word.

CHAPTER 5

'THERE IS NO SUCH THING AS A SEXUAL RELATIONSHIP'

> This natural union of the sexes proceeds according to the mere animal nature (*vaga libido* [unsettled lust], *venus vulgivaga* [roving sexuality], *fornicatio* [fornication]), or according to the law. The latter is marriage (*matrimonium*), which is the union of two persons of different sex for lifelong reciprocal possession of their sexual faculties.
>
> Immanuel Kant, *The Science of Right*

I. When we enter a relationship with another person where the sexual organs (or at least their images) are involved, we believe to be in a sexual relationship. One of the main questions that occupy our minds, however, when we set out to do such a thing, is what *others*, *third parties* will feel, think or say rather than that self-same person. What will our family say? How about our friends? What social status is to be gained (or lost) through such a relationship? What will my ex- (or present) partner/lover/husband/wife will think? And what about that person's ex- (or present) partner/lover/husband/wife? As we can see, although the sexual organs are physically present, their existence is totally overshadowed by language. Everything worthy of note happens in the realm of words and thoughts.

II. The obscene and sexist joke (but wait for the punchline!) goes, a gorgeous and famous woman, possibly a super model (in short, any old female sexual object of desire) and Temel (Temel is the stereotypical *Laz* [people of the Black-Sea coast] who is usually the butt-end of Turkish jokes; replace it with any Cohen, John, Sean, Hans, Pierre) survive a shipwreck and are stranded on a desert island. Since there seems to be no hope of rescue, the woman succumbs to Temel's sexual advances in a short while. But even before the first week is over, Temel falls into a kind of deep sexual apathy; he starts to act coy and reluctant, finds other avenues of interest during daytime, and turns his back and falls asleep at night, most of the time. Since there is an apparent lack of alternatives, the woman starts to drop hints, and after a bit, the hints give way to open demands and finally to downright pleading. She tells him to be open about it and tell her what is missing, what it is that he really wants; because whatever it is, she can provide it, no punches pulled. Temel dismisses her with a shake of the head, saying 'Na-ah, *you* can't do it, no way.' To keep it short, in time, the lady convinces him at least to try it. Temel finds an old suit of clothes from his luggage (which is miraculously saved from the wreck) and dresses the lady as a man. Cuts a piece of her hair and prepares a makeshift moustache for her, and finally looks at the end result with obvious dissatisfaction. Convinced that this is as good as it will ever get, he sits next to her, throws his arm around her shoulders and says: 'Hey Idris (or Goldstein, Angus, George, Johann, or Jacques), can you believe whom I've been fucking this last month?'

III. There is no such thing as a sexual relationship. There is only *the word* about it, that is all.

IV. Going back to the joke, the person who is stranded on a desert island with his object of desire of many years cannot even enjoy it. The circumstances, however, for a 'sexual relationship' as such are apparently perfect: Nothing to hide, no holds barred, nothing to bother the conscience, nobody to interfere. Furthermore, somebody who will not even notice you under different (social) circumstances has no other option but you; they cannot say 'No!' to anything. And it is exactly this isolation, this over-perfection for a 'sexual relationship', this abolition of all other material conditions except *that*, which makes it entirely impossible. Even the simple, comforting illusion that we *need* a sexual relationship in our everyday lives is taken away from us.

V. Because the main element to facilitate that illusion, that is, *a third*, is absent. 'Two's company,' Adam Phillips had said, 'but three's a couple.' (Phillips, *Monogamy*, 94) He was not talking of bigamy or threesomes of course. What he meant was the presence of that eternal third against whom the couple would assert its couple-ness; the third who could both be 'you' and 'him/her', thereby making language possible: the scapegoat; the state, the prohibiting father, the concerned mother, the obscene Master, the *femme fatale*, the womanizing old goat. The Other.

VI. Without the O/other there is no society. And without society there can be no sexual relationship. There can only be copulation; something bees, pigs, cats or salmon can do as well. Admittedly, it is the precondition for reproduction; a chore that befalls gamogenetic entities, mostly animals. Sexual pleasure (but not sexual relationship) is only the incentive for it. It is the carrot at the end of the stick, the reward for obediently doing our chores.

VII. 'Sexual Relationship' is an act we human beings, animals that live not only together but as a social entity, insistently separate from the reproductive function and sublimate; it is peculiar to us alone, something animals do not, cannot, comprehend or acknowledge. It has no natural function, no natural use. It serves neither species nor individual survival.

VIII. The animals, on the other hand, eat, drink, defecate, breathe and copulate. Each of these acts has a natural function. The animal, who doesn't have a function in the continuation of the species, loses the right to exist as well. Haven't we observed the poor male ants countless times, thrashing aimlessly and dying, having lost even the most primitive instinct of self-preservation, after the moment of copulation is over? They have only 48 hours to live from the moment of birth, as opposed to the much longer life-spans of the female albeit sterile drones, and the incredibly longer (sometimes up to decades) life-spans of the queens. Why do the Black Widow and the Praying Mantis females kill and eat the male after the copulation is done? Do we really think it is some kind of a bizarre S&M ritual? In the insect kingdom, the natural function of the male ends after copulation after which it becomes a surplus, excrement in the eco-system; it is left without a purpose other than becoming food for the female, who still has the function of keeping the eggs safe, and taking care of the coming generation.

IX. For centuries, a lot of scientists have spent a lot of ink, paper and general convincing effort to take 'Man' down from the self-appointed pedestal of 'centre of the universe'. We, in our desperate self-centredness, still frantically cling to this imaginary station despite all their efforts. We still struggle to perceive and represent functions peculiar to us human beings as 'natural' functions. This anthropomorphic attitude can be best observed in the field of sexuality and emotions. We project concepts of our own invention like affection, love, lust or compassion, onto poor animals. We think that our cat 'loves' us. We mistake our dog's olfactory addiction for affection. If our two cats (of opposite sexes or the same sex) rub against each other rather than fight, we happily declare on Facebook that they are 'in love'. A mother cat licking her young is immediately accused of 'motherly love', whereas the poor animal is only doing what her instinct dictates: in a year, she will forget about her 'children'.

X. The reproductive instinct drives animals to copulation. We human beings are also driven by the same instinct towards copulation. Unlike animals, however, sexual pleasure, which used to be only a side effect of copulation, becomes for us an end in itself, distinct from reproduction. The only other animal species that even *try* sexual intercourse without copulation are the Bonobos who often practice *coitus interruptus*, and they are so close to *homo sapiens sapiens* both genetically and behaviourally that they should be declared human beings, that is, if they can escape extinction in the next few decades.

XI. Think of all the millennia we have been labouring to have sex without the hazardous 'side' effects of reproduction. The condom has a history of at least three thousand years; pulling back, vaginal wash, intentional miscarriage, abortion (in its primitive and modern forms), and finally the pill and the IUD: the methods we invent to be able to have sex without reproduction will baffle Satan himself, let alone the poor animals.

XII. On the other hand, we spend almost as much effort the other way around, at least recently, to free reproduction from sexuality. Artificial and extra-uterine insemination is commonplace nowadays; surrogate mothers have become a social reality; when extra-uterine foetus growth and birth (a distinct theoretical possibility) becomes an actuality, there will be no connection left to speak of between the two.

XIII. We can conclude, therefore, that sexuality is something solely for human beings; that is, it is social, that is, it is linguistic, that is, it is a game, that is, it is related to consciousness. We have named human beings a lot of things in the past: *Zoon politikon* (city-dwelling animal, social animal), *homo faber* (tool-making human being) *homo ludens* (playing human being), *homo sapiens* (conscious human being), *homo symbolicus* (human being with symbols or with a language). Sexuality is closely related to all these human characteristics: it is a social act; it usually involves tools (from the condom to the pill, from the dildo to all sorts of S&M instruments); it is definitely a game, it is directly linked to consciousness and it definitely cannot exist without language. Copulation and reproduction, on the other hand, do not need any of these. Maybe we can invent/employ a new definition for human beings starting from this hypothesis, *Homo sexualis.*

XIV. Does this burden us with a new complication? I propose that sexuality is a human trait, even a distinguishing trait for human beings, yet I claim that 'there is no such thing as a sexual relationship'. Isn't there a horrible self-contradiction, an oxymoron here?

XV. Well, I will grudgingly admit to a play on words, rather than a self-contradiction. Sexuality of course exists and it remains a major (maybe *the* major) distinguishing trait for human beings; this, however, does not mean that there is such a thing as a 'sexual relationship'.

XVI. Let us take a different approach: Thinking, an act of the intellect, is also a distinguishing trait for human beings. Does this mean that there is such a thing as an 'intellectual relationship'? We are alone in our thoughts, within the bone cage of our skulls; our thoughts belong only to us and they are 'inside'. We have to resort to language in order to convert them into a form of relationship. Without a doubt, we also use 'language' in thinking; but in order to share our thinking, we have to convert it into *utterances,* or, pardon my French, into *énoncés.* The language we use in thinking does not consist of utterings. The *énoncé,* that is, what is actually said, what comes out of our mouths, or pencils and keyboards, and what we *intend to say* are never the same. There is a process of enunciation (*énonciation*) that comes in between, which is free of our conscious intentions and is determined on the one hand by our unconscious, and the limits, rules, conventions and traditions of language on the other.

XVII. Which means that the 'intellectual relationship' we believe to have established is just an illusion. We neither exactly know what we are saying, nor can we exactly understand what we hear from the other party. We usually use the other as a kind of a mirror; an excuse in order to hear our own uttering, or rather, as a puppet. An inevitable puppet of course: without it we would never be able to hear ourselves.

XVIII. Of course our counterpart is no different: haven't you ever been accused of saying something which you haven't said or even thought of saying, during a debate, discussion or fight? The other person was not lying; the 'you puppet', the homunculus representing you in their heads had already said what you were accused of saying. Some people do not listen; they prepare their next speech while you are talking; they make the 'you puppet' in their heads to make the perfect pitch for their next homerun tirade. And why should it sound so outlandish? Did Plato, the inventor of the philosophical form of the 'dialog', do anything much different? Socrates' counterpart in the Platonic discourse is nothing else than a puppet facilitating the 'dialog' ('two-words'); but they are also inevitable. Without them it would only be a monolog.

XIX. Let us replace the 'some people' above with 'all of us, sometimes/usually'. Not because of our evil intentions, our narcissism, our self-worship or our adoration for our own voice; at least *not only*. It is because we cannot do otherwise; because 'intellectual relationship' as such is not possible.

XX. On the other hand, however, we have to create and sustain an illusion of this 'intellectual relationship'; otherwise it would be impossible for us to think. What is the worth of an idea which is not shared, or at least believed to have been shared?

XXI. The same thing is also true for a 'sexual relationship'. In order to make sexuality possible, we need an illusion of a 'sexual relationship'.

XXII. We always think that sexual relationship is something that belongs to the private life, to the intimacy of two people. It is quite the contrary: since sexual intercourse is at most a linguistic misconception, the illusion only begins when one leaves the sphere of private life, of the intimate. Otherwise, why would it be necessary for two people to inform the world of their 'marriage' with fanfares, to announce it in rituals in the church or the temple, wearing specifically designed attires, and with a lot of complicated customs which would seem extremely stupid and childish when viewed from the point of view of another culture?

XXIII. In Turkey, where I hail from, when two people marry they are given a document by the state that practically means 'there is no harm in these people having sexual intercourse'. The authority that issued this document, until some years ago, however, did not have even the slightest relationship with sexuality or sexual intercourse: it was the Ministry of Finance. This again supported my point, that 'there is no such thing as sexual relationship', only a financial and monetary contract. Thank god a Ministry for Pleasure has not (yet) been established! In the eyes of the state, sexuality is nothing more than a by-product of the sharing, handing down and dividing up property.

XXIV. Recently (again in Turkey) the privilege of giving us permission to mate and copulate has been taken from the Ministry of Finance and given to the Ministry of the Interior. Thus, we have succeeded in turning sexual relationship into an issue about crime and security rather than merely a financial problem. Thankfully, there is still no Ministry for Pleasure.

XXV. Things are not much different when sexual relationship is non-contractual: when we speak of a non-contractual sexual relationship, we are referring to either a breach of contract (infidelity, adultery) or a pre-contractual rapport, both of which have to be done more or less in secret, although less and less so in the latter case, at least in the so-called 'free world'. Since 'secret' means *mystikos* in classical Greek, there is again a 'mystical' element in the 'sexual relationship', although of a different sort.

XXVI. So, 'sexual relationship' must be socialized by either declaring it with fanfare or keeping it secret. In other words, it has to be *named*: marriage, secret love, deception, a fleeting adventure, a one-night stand, eternal love, etc. Adam Phillips says: 'And yet the fetish most people need is often simply the name of the relationship, its official title. The problem —or, indeed the pleasure— of a marriage is that it can never be called an affair. If the word doesn't fit then the genitals won't either.' (Phillips, *Monogamy*, 83)

XXVII. Nancy in *Bananas*, who turned Fielding Mellish's life into a nightmare by insisting that 'Something is missing,' eventually agrees to marry him, although the lack is still there. The wedding night of this marriage, however, will be broadcast live on television. Aside from being a precise prediction of today's tendency in TV to publicize the most banal aspects of private life, it is important to observe here the determination that sexual relationship should be *socialized* in order to function, rather than the prophecy itself.

XXVIII. Once the sexual 'relationship' has been named and socialized, it becomes an object of desire that exists in and for itself. It becomes desirable for its name and the *form* of social relationship it implies, rather than the sexuality it implicates and sanctions, or for the pleasure to be obtained thereof.

XXIX. And precisely for this reason it is no longer *accessible*. Once established, it is nothing but 'Ah, he/she wasn't "the one",' or 'Wait, is that it?' or 'Well, thank goodness for small favours.'

XXX. Sexual relationship becomes (or seems to be) the cure for that irreplaceable lack, that insatiable drought, that transcendental loneliness, in short, the catastrophe of having been born, something that has always existed in all of us, from the very beginning. It leads us to think that we have re-found our mother, not our actual, flesh and blood mother, but the entity that comforted us a little when we first woke up to our loneliness, that created the illusion that we are *included*, that we are incorporated into something larger than our pitiful bodies. Like most drugs, however, it does not heal but only relieves the symptoms, and that, only for a fleeting moment.

XXXI. Every person who needs or wants a sexual relationship, first desires the relationship itself, not the partner with whom they (will) have intercourse with; not *the other*. The other is just a material necessity for the relationship to exist. We can't have intercourse with an absence, can we? 'Sexual relationship' is transcendental, it has no taste, smell, colour, touch or sound. In its featurelessness, in its function as a universal substitute, it can replace *the other*, which we think we lost at the moment of birth, that other we do not even know what it is, which is identical to the 'I'. Whereas a partner has (a) character (at least *characteristics*). They have taste, smell, colour, touch or a voice. They are *themselves*, and as such they cannot replace the featureless and amorphous lack we desperately desire.

XXXII. When choosing a 'partner' for ourselves, we choose them with their idiosyncrasies, peculiarities and oddities, in their uniqueness which distinguish them from other 'suitable candidates'. In order for us to desire them, we must find a 'difference' that will trigger our desire. But once a relationship is established, our partners usually prove to be quite disappointing. They spoil our illusions and prevent us from deceiving ourselves. That's why every sexual relationship necessarily ends one day, although its name, its social status, or the compulsory routines it brings along does not necessarily end.

XXXIII. Every partner is a screen. On that screen we reflect the fantasy of our desire, and we establish a relationship with this reflection. Of course, what we are projecting is nothing other than ourselves. Therefore, every sexual relationship is an act of absolute narcissism. It is an admirably camouflaged masturbation, the epitome of incest.

XXXIV. The 'emptier' our partner's surface that functions as a screen is, the more successful the relationship will be. The unevenness of the surface (idiosyncrasies, distinctive features, flaws) disturbs our peace, and over time it begins to offend our eyes, irritate us. Those flaws, however, were the precisely the reason why we chose that partner in the first place, because they distinguished them from the others.

XXXV. Many men openly or secretly want a virgin to have a lasting sexual relationship. A significant number of gays and lesbians (at least in their fantasies) want to seduce straight people; most women have a desire (again, at least fantastically) for a knight in shining armour. And all these desires last only until they are fully satisfied. As soon as we conquer the virgin, she is no longer a virgin. The moment we seduce the heterosexual, they are no longer straight; and the moment the knight in shining armour (as we have already seen in Chapter 2) has sexual intercourse, he leaves the courtly love matrix and turns into a real, tangible man, a rapist bully from actual medieval history.

XXXVI. Desire is directed precisely at what our desire will destroy. In this sense, sexual relationship begins when the desire is satisfied and ends at the same time, since satisfaction removes the object of desire.

XXXVII. So, just as there is no single sexual relationship, there is no long-term institutionalized sexual relationship either. The illusion of this latter, however, is easier to establish and to maintain; it is socially and culturally more efficient.

XXXVIII. It can, for instance, facilitate the emergence of a concept called 'love', and we cannot easily say 'there is no such thing as love', although we can proclaim that '*Il n'y a pas d'amour heureux,*' as the poet Aragon convincingly argued. On the contrary, there is a lot of evidence that there exists such a thing as 'love', as an illusion of sublimated sexual intercourse, and, fortunately for our sanity, there is a lot of it to go around.

XXXIX. Talking about love, Lacan says, 'Love is to give what one does not have to someone who does not want it.' (Lacan, *Seminar XII*) Sounds like a pathetic situation, right? There is nothing to be given, but no one wants it anyway. But all the same, 'love' still exists. Because whoever that other person is, nobody gets what they 'really' want. If somebody had, what could they have given in return?

XL. So love is an exchange of illusions; an 'as if' endeavour. We should not, however, just say 'as if' and leave it there: isn't what we call art also an 'as if' endeavour, a pretension, a copy without an original? Although we cannot observe the 'finally found' love around us in our everyday lives, and much less, a case of 'happy love', we all know very well about love-turned-into-art. This means that love has meaning even if it is not really there: a significance that supersedes existence.

XLI. And, by the way, let us not be too hasty in insulting love, calling it a *mere* illusion. What is not an illusion in our lives anyway? Love may not be real, but may very well give us a glimpse into Truth.

XLII. The fate of cynics, on the other hand, who are not 'taken in' by such illusions, is even more pathetic. They know that sexual relationship is 'merely' an illusion, that love is also a misconception, and, of course, they proudly declare, they don't believe in such drivel. This is why they can never keep out of trouble.

XLIII. Let us refer to Adam Phillips again: 'Only the cynic knows the future because he has seen it all before. For the omniscient sex is always a problem.' (Phillips, *Monogamy*, 95)

XLIV. The cynics have seen every movie before, read every novel before, experienced every love before; Therefore, no sane director would attempt to make a film for the cynics, and no self-respecting novelist would write a novel for them.

XLV. Perhaps there will be a few people who will manage to fall in love with the cynic, duped by the shiny, smooth surface of cynicism, or at least admire them and mistake this admiration for love. But fortunately, that love will only last until they scrape the surface. If you scrape the surface of a cynic, what will you find underneath? As Cordelia, the party girl gradually becoming a wise woman from the TV series *Angel* would say, 'More surface.'

CHAPTER 6

~~THE WO~~MAN DOES NOT EXIST ANYHOW

> To Sherlock Holmes she is always the woman. I have seldom heard him mention her under any other name. In his eyes she eclipses and predominates the whole of her sex. It was not that he felt any emotion akin to love for Irene Adler. All emotions, and that one particularly, were abhorrent to his cold, precise but admirably balanced mind.
>
> A. Conan Doyle, *A Scandal in Bohemia*

I. Duygu Asena, a quite popular Turkish feminist, once wrote a novel (actually two of them) titled, *The Woman Has No Name*. She was right. The woman truly has no name; how can something that does not exist ever have a name?

II. Lacan said, '~~The wo~~man does not exist'. Things, however, are a little more complicated in this statement than it first seems: the original phrase in French is '~~La~~ *femme n'existe pas*', but it is a sentence that pushes at the boundaries of written language, because the '~~La~~' is crossed out. When translated into English, the phrase becomes '~~The wo~~man does not exist', which does not quite do justice to the word-play in the original, because the definite article which is feminine in French becomes neutral in English, leaving out half of the word-play.

III. So instead of translating Lacan's sentence directly into English, we try to convey its meaning in different ways. Some translate it as, 'There is no such thing as "The Woman"'. What I understand from Lacan, however, is: 'Woman cannot be *determined*.' Or, more precisely, 'There is no such thing as 'the Woman', as a determinable/delimitable entity.' The bar in the original not only deletes femininity, but also determinability. In English I try to match this by not only barring the 'the', but also the 'wo' in 'woman' to convey both meanings, but this is only a pale attempt at replicating the semantic profundity of Lacan's original statement.

IV. The statement, when it was first made, had immediately become the target of (some) feminist critics: What do you mean? Women *do* exist! Here we are! They were of course deceived by Lacan's rather freely phrased expression, without (one has to admit) much regard for his audience, cherishing brevity and clever word-play at the expense of comprehensibility. Of course there are *women*; fortunately for all of us, they *do* exist. What Lacan asserted was that women cannot be completely determined and delimited, and hence *subjectified* by/in language, which is first and foremost a male construct. Unlike men, there is the notorious Lacanian *'pas-tout'* (not-all/whole) in women that escapes determination: in Lacan's logical symbolism, $\overline{\forall}x\Phi x$, which can be translated into common speech as 'not all (of the) wom(a/e)n is/are subject to the phallic function'.

V. If language is something men (had) construct(ed) and shape(d), every characterisation, every designation made using it tends to be 'by men and for men'. As such, attributing determinacy to 'the woman' means subjecting her to/within a primarily male- (or father-) dominated symbolic system. Lacan's statement, then, that ~~the wo~~man does not exist' actually serves to *free* the woman from this certainty, or more precisely, this 'determination'. Once the woman is fully determined within language, she becomes an object *for* men. The possibility of escaping this determination (even partially), on the other hand, opens up a space of freedom for them. This space, however, is undefined, unstructured, nebulous; but doesn't one of the many meanings of freedom lie in the lack/inability or definition and delimitation?

VI. It is a shortcut to assert that language is a 'man-made' thing, but it is easier said than demonstrated. Structurally, the existence of linguistic gender discrimination, especially in European languages, supports this claim; but the absence of the same discrimination in some other (mainly Eastern) languages such as Turkish or Japanese complicates things. When you speak of an indeterminate person in a profession or position (say, a doctor) in English, you refer to it as 'he' (masculine third person singular) in your second sentence. The uncertain 'human' is always male. In French, a group of people will be referred to as *'ils'* (masculine 'they') even if there is only one male in it; that group will never be *'elles'* unless and until they get rid of this troublemaking male among them. Feminists have been trying to challenge this for decades, but unfortunately language is much more resilient than social institutions. You can change the laws, but you cannot readily change the language at will.

VII. Neurologically, there is no fundamental difference between the linguistic abilities of women and men. From a historical point of view, however, if we consider that the tasks that require both tool use and group coordination such as hunting in pre-Neolithic times mainly fall to share of men, we can say that this claim has some sort of a foundation in the anthropological and evolutionary facts we have in hand. Women in this scheme are left with jobs that do not require much linguistic communication, such as childcare, which is primarily pre-linguistic, since the infant and the caregiver (most of the time the genetic mother) are still in empathic rapport. Another activity that falls to the women's lot in this pre-Neolithic division of labour, gathering, usually does not need much group coordination either; it is something done together, but without a discernible hierarchy and division of labour within the group.

VIII. Another evidence that language is fundamentally masculine is that we have used the terms 'human' and 'man' synonymously for centuries, even millennia. Even Turkish, which is free of gendered pronouns and articles, names 'humanity' as '*insanoğlu*'— the son of man. The 'talking animal' is, then, more often than not, a man.

IX. In English, 'Mankind' means 'Humanity'. In 1789, what the French revolutionaries announced was not the 'Universal Declaration of Human Rights' but the 'Universal Declaration of Man's Rights' (*Déclaration universelle des droits de l'homme*).

X. 'Man' as a supposedly neuter determination is still male; because it was men who defined the concept of 'humanity' first. Marx and Engels had asserted in the *German Ideology*, that 'Men can be distinguished from animals by consciousness, by religion or anything else you like. They themselves begin to distinguish themselves from animals as soon as they begin to produce their means of subsistence, a step which is conditioned by their physical organisation.' (Marx & Engels, *The German Ideology*) When they try to distinguish human beings from animals, even the founders of Communism resort to a male-defined and defined-as-male 'humanity'. To be perfectly fair, the actual term they use is '*Menschen*' rather than '*Männer*', but this may only be splitting hairs: '*der Mensch*' is also rooted in '*der Mann*' after all; it is still etymologically masculine and structurally excludes women.

XI. If, however, we leave aside the male-dominated burden of language, and take Marx and Engels' words at face value, we can see that *people* separate themselves from animals when they start producing their means of subsistence. Since the social/economic period that immediately follows this is based upon the private appropriation of the means of production by *men* (we have arrived at the Neolithic now and have better documentation to make sure that it is actually the case), it is not surprising that this distinction, that is, the conceptualization of 'humanity', is made by *men*. When they mean 'human' they say *men*, meaning themselves.

XII. Language is also structurally masculine because it is shaped and first learned in a nuclear structure that is pertinent for almost the entirety of the universal concept we call humanity. This structure is the family; that is, its most recent version which is strictly triangular, shaped by the addition of a man we will later call 'father', a third element, to the mother-child relationship, which is not dependent on language and belongs to a pre-linguistic universe.

XIII. Undoubtedly, the family I am talking about here is merely an abstraction. The Judeo-Christian nuclear family, which is the source of Freud's 'Oedipal' triangle, is neither the first nor the 'essential' form of the family. As seventeenth-century European capitalism became the dominant socio-economic form, however, first for Europe and eventually for the whole world, this family structure also became universalised. In attaining universality, it not only destroyed the cultural and historical features of many different forms of the hitherto existing family, but also incorporated, devoured and assimilated most of them. As a result, the dominant family form of the nineteenth and twentieth centuries also includes the most basic features of family structures in different periods and cultures throughout human history.

XIV. This 'universalised' family is built on two basic assumptions: the prohibition of incest and the mandatory monogamy of women. These two prohibitions are the constituent elements of not only family but also of male- (or father-) domination in general, in diverse cultures and societies throughout history.

XV. The incest ban or taboo is supposed to prohibit sexual intercourse between first-degree relatives (parents/children and siblings). This common-sense assertion, however, is not entirely correct. There are actually three distinct prohibitions included in the incest taboo: The prohibition of sexual intercourse between siblings; the prohibition of sexual intercourse between father and children; and the prohibition of sexual intercourse between mother and children.

XVI. The prohibition of sexual intercourse between siblings is not one of the founding injunctions of the family. It is not insistently scrutinised and supervised, and most of the time ignored—unless the siblings openly declare it or try to make it official. Even then, in relatively 'recent' civilizations such as Ancient Egypt (only 3-4 millennia ago), noble families encouraged rather than banned sibling marriages (even marriages with the father in rare cases) in order to keep the property within the family. In terms of childhood sexuality, it is an embarrassment for the parents if siblings engage in pre-pubertal sexual game-play, but it is not a deadly sin, a ban that must be enforced at all costs. In the mythology of polytheistic religions, there is frequent flirtation and sexual rapport between sibling gods. King Arthur's son Mordred was born to his sister Morgana. In the Old Testament, which is the founding text of monotheistic religions, all humanity originates from sibling incest, even if it is not explicitly stated: where did the wives of Abel and Cain, the ancestors of all of us, come from? Since Adam and Eve were the first (and only) human beings, and there were no other people in the world other than Adam, Eve, Abel, and Cain, shouldn't their wives also be the children of Adam and Eve?

XVII. The prohibition of sexual intercourse between father and children is not a serious injunction either, albeit a little bit more serious and frowned-upon than the one between siblings. Again, in the Old Testament, for instance, Lot's sexual intercourse with his daughters is treated not as a sin that deserves divine punishment, although it is not exactly sanctioned. In the same chapter where Lot's incest was slurred over, however, as something necessary but not to be proud of, homosexuality was treated as a sin so grave that an entire city was destroyed by a 'rain of sulphur and fire'.

XVIII. As of today, fathers' harassment and/or rape of their daughters (and not infrequently sons) are becoming more common, although harassment and rape of minors are considered crimes. Undoubtedly, the problem is not (only) that is becoming more widespread, but (also) that the children are more enabled to speak about them candidly. Especially in the UK and the USA, the number of fathers facing this accusation is constantly increasing; because children can now somehow trust that they will be protected by the state when they disclose what happens 'within the family'. Father harassment and abuse, however, are still treated mostly as misdemeanours rather than crimes, being still kept within the family institution as an exception, but not an integral feature of the structure itself. Of course, the law punishes the excessively abusive fathers from time to time, if he goes 'too far', albeit not for 'incest' as such, but for the more ordinary crimes of harassment or rape.

XIX. Because the prohibition of incest is not exactly a *legal* prohibition. In fact, it's not even a verbalised, pronounced taboo. It is a pre-linguistic ban. Who remembers *having been told* that sexual intercourse with our mother, father or siblings is prohibited? Probably nobody, because it is not usually said out loud, which drives many people to assume that we were *born* with this information, that it is not acquired, but a natural or God-given knowledge.

XX. What is left, then, is the prohibition of incest between mother and son. Now, this is where things go instantaneously serious: Mother-son sexual intercourse is definitely not tolerable; it is an 'unmentionable'. Although sexual intercourse between siblings or between father and daughter can be tolerated, ignored, or glossed over, claiming that it is an exception rather than the rule, mother-son incest immediately goes beyond the limits of everyone's tolerance.

XXI. Only once in the history of art and literature (at least until the 20th century) we come across a serious depiction of mother-son incest: Sophocles' tragedy of *Oedipus Tyrannus*, where it is treated as a major catastrophe and will become the curse of a whole lineage and an entire city. This single act of incest, although committed unknowingly and hence quite innocently, starts the entire process of destruction that reaches all the way to the tragedy of *Antigone*. On the other hand, Oedipus, becomes one of the basic concepts and cornerstones of contemporary psychoanalysis: Were it not for (the) Oedipus (Complex), by what would we remember Freud?

XXII. Oedipus' mother incest (which he unknowingly commits) is both the source and result of a curse that have lasted, and will last for generations to come: Oedipus will blind himself, his sons born from the union with his mother will kill each other, and his daughter Antigone will be buried alive. In the seventeenth century, when John Milton attempted the colossal task of incorporating almost all of humanity's mythological stories into Christian mythology in his *Paradise Lost*, he gave birth to *Sin* from Lucifer's head, just as Athena was born from Zeus's head. *Death* arises from Sin's mating with his father, and *Death* in turn mates with his mother, from which *Hell-Hounds* will breed.

XXIII. One of the most important representations of mother-son incest in contemporary literature that I know of is Bataille's novel *Ma Mère* and Christophe Honoré's film adapted from this novel. But isn't Bataille famous for such eccentric challenges? Apart from this, mother-son incest can be found in late twentieth century Japanese literature and Manga, but this also causes a sense of dread in popular media.

XXIV. Undoubtedly, the same prohibition also applies to the sexual relationship between mother and daughter, but it does not 'deserve' the same scandalous attention, because the mother-daughter sexual relationship falls victim to heterosexist voluntary blindness towards lesbianism *before* it violates the incest ban. Since sexual rapport between two women does not involve a penis (at least a flesh and blood one), the popular attitude is willing to disregard it as 'sex', so it can be neglected in all its forms, unless and until it 'advertises' itself.

XXV. One of the more or less understandable explanations for the prohibition of incest is the prevention of the survival and expansion of recessive genetic disorders. Of course, this was not because our ancestors of tens of thousands of years ago were genetic experts. Probably tens, even hundreds of thousands of years before the time of the prohibition, the law of natural selection was still fully operational for the human race, and communities that did not enforce this prohibition were more susceptible to genetic degradation than those that did, and eventually dissolved.

XXVI. This explanation alone does not explain, however, the prohibition of incest in all its incarnations. First of all, it does not reasonably explain why incestuous relationships between mother-child (horrible), father-child (shame and disgrace) and sibling-sibling (better ignored) are subject to a hierarchy, and occupy quite different places throughout cultures, since genetically all three represent the same level of threat.

XXVII. Another and non-genetic explanation for the prohibition of sexual intercourse between mother and child may be as follows: During the period between birth and the infant's entry in the 'symbolic order', that is, its learning the language, mother and child experience a relationship that is almost as close as 'unity', a kind of symbiosis which does not involve language, but based on empathy. If children later channel all their emotional investment towards their mother and try to meet all their desires and needs (including sexual ones, albeit in disguise) from the mother, they will regress to and/or be fixed in this pre-linguistic/pre-semantic region. They cannot be socialized, cannot be integrated within culture. If the circumstances of the first two years of the mother-child relationship extends to the entire life of the child, it usually ends up in psychosis, and a socially dysfunctional non-individual.

XXVIII. The case of Norman Bates in Hitchcock's film *Psycho*, already mentioned before, narrates what happens if the child could not separate from the mother, and could not form a 'self' with its own definite psychic limits. They don't comprehend where the mother ends and where they begin. Therefore, even after the mother dies, they will try to keep her *inside* (symbolically, 'at home'), in body and soul. They will not be able to break away from their mother and therefore cannot be a person, an 'I'.

XXIX. The reason for the prohibition of incest, and especially the mother-child incest, is that it facilitates the separation of the child from the mother. Humanity and society can only evolve further *after* this separation is realised and the child achieves the potential of becoming an individual. Again, this did not happen because at some point in history our ancestors became expert psychoanalysts, and duly prohibited incest. It was because communities that forewent this taboo did not have the chance to develop as a culture and eventually a society, while others did, and successfully established a culture/civilisation of neurotics.

XXX. Language is what separates the child from the mother. The child's learning the language and the father's entry into its life as an instituting element, happen almost simultaneously. To be sure, it is not the necessarily the *genetic* father we are talking about: it can be any authority figure that is introduced into the closed binary structure of the mother-child relationship and breaks this unity, separating the child from the mother. In some cultures, this figure may be an uncle (maternal or paternal). If there is none, even a grandmother representing the father will do. If we don't have even that, the state, your friendly police officer, the village *imam*, or the orphanage supervisor will undertake that function. Anybody, any institution, *but* the mother.

XXXI. I have asserted that that children are separated from mothers by language. Boys are not likely to return to the magical, speechless, empathetic world of mother-child symbiosis. They will forever be sentenced to live in the prison of language, devised, regulated and ruled by men.

XXXII. Girls, on the other hand, may return to the magical world of pre-linguistic existence, several times if they so choose: by becoming mothers. They will experience the mother-child relationship, this time from the *other* position, but as empathetic and as magical.

XXXIII. It is precisely for this reason that women are not as captive to language as men are. Of course, language enslaves women more strictly than it does men. That crack, however, that fissure through which women are temporarily able to escape to (at least glimpse at) an extra-linguistic existence, does not exist for men.

XXXIV. This is, of course, an incomplete escape, because it is also an escape from society, from culture. Most women do not do this on purpose. On the contrary, it is usually forced on them by the father-dominant order, which endeavours to 'keep' women pregnant at all times so that they cannot even contemplate another life: it needs this, because it desperately strives to 'continue the bloodline' and 'hand down the property'. As a result, women miss most opportunities to become independent individuals by constantly giving birth to and caring for children. But unknowingly and unwillingly, every time they give birth to a child, they temporarily escape to a place where men are not (not-yet and not-anymore) predominant.

XXXV. Some second-generation feminists of the 1960s and 70s were surely retreating from a radical position when they began to talk about the virtues and advantages of 'female nature' and 'being a mother' in the 1980s: they helped essentialise a social and cultural paradox by reducing it to a biological difference. Might some of them, however, have at least sensed the escape route I just tried to describe in this retreat?

XXXVI. ~~The wo~~man does not exist. There are infant girls, young girls, mothers, infertile women, childless women by choice, prostitutes, trans women, *femmes fatale*, crones. 'The woman' is many different things at the same time. Men who try to squeeze her into a general category of 'the woman' (as I also do occasionally albeit unwillingly) and women who readily accept this definition/limitation and start speaking as a representative of 'the woman', are ultimately serving the father-dominant order.

XXXVII. 'The man' exists, because since Capitalism established the concept of 'Human' as a universal concept during the Enlightenment, it could not be anything but a 'man': male, white, bourgeois. 'The man' (*L'homme*), therefore, exists as a definable, delimitable concept; at least, *until* some men realize that being 'the man' is as much of an enslavement as being 'the woman', or sometimes even more, and start looking for a crack, a gap, a way out of the symbolic order that imprisons them within the confines of their 'cherished' masculinity.

XXXVIII. The concept of 'the woman' emerges when it becomes necessary to name and subjectivise beings that are 'alike but not quite'; beings that are supposed to be accepted as 'human' but do not exactly resemble men. And this would only be possible after the 'Universal Declaration of *Man's* Rights' is proclaimed, and four years later, Olympe de Gouges is sent to the guillotine by the Jacobins for publishing '*Déclaration des droits de la femme et de la citoyenne*' (Declaration of the Rights of the Woman and of the [Female] Citizen). What else did we expect from the Jacobins, anyhow, whose 'human rights' are only 'men's rights', and when they say *fraternité* (brotherhood) they mean exactly that: the solidarity of men excluding women?

XXXIX. It was indeed the Jacobins themselves, the *bona fide* representatives of the coming world order, who crossed out the '*la*' in the '*des droits de la femme*' when they sent de Gouges to the guillotine, and Lacan's bar crossing out the '*la*' also represents the guillotine's blade in this instance.

XL. Woman *is* the property and the slave of man. Woman *was* the property and the slave of man. Woman is *not entirely* the property and the slave of the man; *not anymore*. Woman is *not yet entirely* emancipated from being the property and the slave of the man. Thus, women have not been able to name themselves as different categories, individuals, identities. That's why we all agreed with Duygu Asena when she said 'The Woman Has No Name'. The woman's name may potentially exist, in the struggle for emancipation, but it is *not yet*.

XLI. When Lacan said, 'T̶h̶e̶ ̶w̶oman does not exist', he infuriated many feminists. What he really told us, however, was that it was the necessary emancipatory step to refuse to be trapped in the category of 'the woman', an invention of men. There are no women: there are female children, young girls, fertile or non-fertile women, mothers, women who refuse to be mothers, trans women, old wives, crones, prostitutes, free women, lesbians. When all these are put together, the ensuing whole is something more (and/or less) than 'the woman'.

XLII. It is more, because the determination 'the woman' that we create by bringing together and delimiting different human individuals and groups, does not contain the possibilities of emancipation from this determination, this limitation itself. *Before* the definition of 'the woman', however, *prior to* this linguistic determination, there is always a way of escape from it: a crack, a gap: 'There is a crack in everything,' says Leonard Cohen (*Anthem*, 1992), 'That's how the light comes in.' The generalization of 'the woman' does not include this way out, this crack, this possibility of emancipation. Therefore, 'women' are *more than* 'the woman'.

XLIII. It is less, because the generalization/determination of 'the woman' adds a surplus, an excess over this whole. This 'excess' represents a strict hierarchy, a relationship of domination, as is the case with all social surpluses. When you assemble and designate all people who lack a 'Y' chromosome or a penis as a category, you also place them in an assigned position within a relationship of domination. This way, you identify them with a lack (a missing penis or a 'Y' chromosome) from the very beginning and create an over-determination from that lack.

XLIV. On the other hand, the argument that the determination of 'the woman' also has a positive 'excess' (i.e. a uterus), is quite suspect. The women who do not use this uterus (women without children by choice), who have lost it (women who underwent total hysterectomy), whose uterus is dysfunctional (infertile women), or who do not have it at all (trans women), are not, or at least should not be excluded from the determination of 'the woman'.

XLV. The eunuch, on the other hand, the man who involuntarily loses his penis and testicles is usually left out of the determination of 'the man'. From the viewpoint of the father-dominant order, he gains a special status as a 'eunuch', also designating a specific social function, albeit, fortunately, an almost extinct one. When this 'loss' is voluntary, as in the case of a male-to-female trans person, she is inscribed on the 'woman's side', albeit reluctantly, but still considered by many (e.g. the 'Trans-Exclusive Radical Feminists') as 'less than women', thus creating a new assigned 'lower' position within the already existing hierarchical relationship of domination.

XLVI. ~~The wo~~man does not exist', but women do. Moreover, they are better equipped than men for emancipation. They neither have to create a new language of their own, a 'women's language' for emancipation, as Luce Irigaray had suggested, nor must they prove that they can use language better than men (that is, they can also be masters in the symbolic order). They are better equipped, because they can remember, albeit vaguely, ambiguously, fragmentarily what existed *before* language, and hence they have a better chance than men to imagine what might exist *outside and beyond* language, and to sublate (*aufheben*) language on the basis of this knowledge.

XLVII. ~~The wo~~man does not exist', but 'the man' does. Those of us who still identify as men but need to get out from under the crushing weight of 'masculinity', should learn to suspend the commanding presence of masculine language, in order to pay attention to what women hear from beyond language in fragments and try to communicate to us all, sometimes without verbalizing. How are we going to manage this? Lacan tells us that, 'It is expressly stated in Freudian theory, that all speaking beings, whoever they be and whether or not they are provided with the attributes of masculinity [...] are allowed to inscribe themselves on this [woman's] side.' (Lacan 1982, *Feminine Sexuality*, 150)

CHAPTER 7

SILENTIUM UNIVERSI

> Last of all, gentlemen: it is best to do nothing! The best thing is conscious inertia! So long live the underground! Although I have said that I am green with envy of the normal man, I wouldn't like to be him in the circumstances in which I see him (even though I shall not cease to envy him, all the same). No, no, the underground is better, in any case. There one can at least.... Ach! The fact is I'm lying even now! I'm lying, because I know, as sure as two and two make four, that it isn't the underground that is better, but something different, entirely different, which I am eager for, but 'which I shall never find. Devil take the underground!
>
> Fyodor Dostoyevsky. *Notes from Underground*

I. Is the universe really silent? There are billions of stars, billions of planets, quasars, black holes and neutron stars out there. Shouldn't they make a tremendous noise as each one of them went their own way? But we still call the universe 'silent'. Why not 'dark'? Most of the cosmos is as dark as it is quiet after all; only we cannot hear all of its sounds and see all its light. Sound does not travel through the void, but it still manages to reach us by transforming into radio waves or cosmic waves. We prefer, however, to explain what is missing in the universe (what is missing *for us*) with our sense of hearing rather than our sense of sight. Yet isn't human culture predominantly visual? Don't we just ground everything on our sense of vision? So why do we define a very important and vital element of the universe that we feel missing with 'silence'? It must be from the metaphorical relationship that 'sound' establishes with meaning. Otherwise, an infinite amount of sounds, 'voices', come to us from the universe; The only problem is that we cannot *make sense* of them.

II. James Gunn tells us the story of a group of people 'listening' to space with giant space telescopes in *The Listeners* (short story 1968, novel 1972). There is a constant white noise, a rustle, but what they expect is a message, a declaration of '*Sum!* — I exist!' We constantly expect news that will break the feeling that we are alone in the universe. After all, what is that 'loneliness' other than a megalomaniac, sublime manifestation of our individual loneliness? The universe, however, remains indifferent to us. It makes a lot of sounds but does not speak to us—at least in a language we can understand.

III. However, if someone/something out there would actually say, 'I exist!', we would deduce from that message, from this very announcement, that they could *think* ('*Loqui quod sum ergo cogito!* — I say I exist; therefore, I think!'), that they were *like us*, our infinitely aggrandised analogues on a cosmic scale. This is what the 'listeners' expect: to find a gigantic, cosmic-sized mirror, rather than to hear a *bona fide* 'other'. As long as this turns out to be a futile expectation, we get the feeling that there is something 'missing' in the universe. The only thing missing, however, is a mirror for us. The Mother. The Phallus.

IV. Stanislaw Lem, Science-Fiction writer, philosopher, and cosmologist *par excellence*, is probably one of those thinkers who contemplate most about the *Silentium Universi*, on the silence of the universe. In his masterpiece *Solaris* (1961), he describes a vibrant and conscious (?) ocean that covers the surface of an entire planet. The ocean is 'one', so it has never experienced the concept of communication; there is no other entity to communicate *with*. So, the silence of the universe is absolute for this ocean. But one day people from Earth arrive and try to extricate a message from the sheer presence and movements of this ocean. They try to 'hear' it. The ocean, on the other hand, has just encountered another being other than itself for the first time. It does not even try to convey a message or anything like it. It doesn't even 'know' what a message is. The only thing it does to these tiny creatures that roam over its surface, is to reach out to their minds, get hold of their deepest, most secret desires and fears, and make them become real. The only reaction those 'realised' unattainable desires create in human beings, however, is sheer horror. The protagonist of the novel, Kelvin, cannot forget his wife, who committed suicide some years ago; he misses her and constantly suffers a profound guilt feeling over her suicide. The ocean gives him his wife, complete, but only as she exists in his memory. An important part of the novel is about Kelvin's attempt to *destroy* this 'gift'.

V. In short, if the universe actually sent us a voice, we would desperately try *not* to hear that voice, and, if we could not succeed in doing that, we would try to destroy its source. This is why most 'First Contact' stories in Science-Fiction eventually end up in violence. The precondition for the existence of the *objet petit a*, the object of desire, is that it must remain unattained.

VI. It is not an arbitrary choice that Lem's Solaris is an ocean: in our collective imagination, the ocean represents infinity, absolute inclusion. Therefore, it actually corresponds to the earliest stage in the development of the individual, a moment when the universe was not divided into 'I' and 'the external world'; to the moment when we were whole with the mother (and with the whole universe through her); when we were not restricted by language and its prohibitions; when we could not see ourselves in the mirror and recognize ourselves as the 'I'. It corresponds to 'The Real'. There is no meaning in the ocean, although it is not senseless.

VII. The lack of signification that condemns us to inaction when confronted with that ocean, also corresponds to the absence of the phallus. Just as we keep trying to create for us a phallus all through our lives, something that will enable us, give us power, but unfortunately does not exist, we will try to ascribe meaning to things that do not speak to us or respond to our futile attempts at communication. This is the price of having been born.

VIII. Every meaning we manage to attribute to 'the Real', to that vast presence encircling and engulfing us, but without any meaning, intention or purpose, will give us a crumb of power. The impossibility of signification, on the other hand, implies a total lack of power: helplessness, inaction, catatonia. This is the problem for all of us, men and women alike, whether temporary or permanent, partial or total: Impotence.

IX. Impotence, lack of power. The other extreme immediately comes to mind: Omnipotence, all-powerfulness. Let's leave aside the petty physical impotence of a small number of men (which should better be called erectile dysfunction). Actually, what is impotence, no matter whether in men or women, other than a broken, incomplete omnipotence, 'a cold and broken Hallelujah'? If I can't move the earth with my phallus, since my phallus is not, and will never be, a big enough lever, what good is an erection?

X. We believe that our existence should be like our phallus. If there is no answer to our atomic beings from the whole universe (*since* such an answer will not come), it is just as well we do not exist at all. The answers given to us by other atoms, entities like ourselves, do not matter.

XI. The (unrealisable) desire of the atom is to come face to face with the whole, to see itself in the mirror of the totality of the cosmos. Atoms ignore other atoms as insignificant, although it is *them* that make the cosmos whole.

XII. But what is this 'whole'? Where does it reside? Most of us are doubtful (with justification) about the 'truth' of what those around us constantly peddle, persistently announcing, 'Here is the whole, here is the universe, here is the absolute truth!' So, we adopt a sceptical, even cynical attitude towards these self-professed proclamations. But at the same time, many of us are afraid of preaching *our* whole, *our* own universe, *our* own absolute truths against them. Because we are painfully aware that such claims are worthy of faith only when they are not put into actual words. If they were, they would be the target of the same unbelieving, critical, cynical attitude. Or, less likely but even worse, some will believe in the absolute truths we preach, and they will follow us, saying, like the guy in the Nasreddin Hodja story, who was sawing off the branch he was sitting on, 'Hodja, you predicted I was going to fall, so you must know when I will die.' They will thus lock us in the absolute of our own belief and thought.

XIII. Groucho Marx, one of the greatest psychoanalytical thinkers of the twentieth century, says 'I don't want to belong to any club that will accept me as a member.' Adam Phillips, another great psychoanalytical thinker of the twentieth century, says 'There can be no life without violence because all violence is the violence of exclusion.' (Phillips, *Monogamy*, 113) When considered together, don't these two quotations tell us that those who cannot give up violence, will deliberately choose to stay out when faced with a situation that does not necessarily exclude them, because that inclusion would have put an end to the only manner of existence they have ever learned, violence? Groucho Marx's amazing insight tells us, 'I am such a sublime being that I would not bother to join a group that could include a vile creature like me.'

XIV. Supreme being and vile creature. Me and Me. In an episode of *Star Trek* ('The Alternative Factor', Season 1, Episode 27, 1967), two aspects of the same creature, one 'good' and the other 'evil' (one 'matter' and the other 'anti-matter') are locked up in a chase that devastates planets and stars. The moment they meet, the entire universe will disappear (if matter and anti-matter come together in the same time and space, it negates existence). Fortunately, practical Captain Kirk and logical Mister Spock devise a plan to imprison these two creatures in a contained and locked 'time tunnel' so they can fight each other forever without harming anyone. Unfortunately, in this ordinary universe without Captain Kirk and Mister Spock, the wars between I and I wreak havoc on everyone in our immediate (and, depending on how much actual, this-worldly power we possess, extended) environment.

XV. There is no end to the war between the need to belong (return to the womb, inclusion, acceptance, flattery), which is one of the most basic needs in all of us, and the Marx Paradox ('I don't want to belong to any club that will accept me as a member'). And this is where all the violence comes out of. Either an extrapunitive violence, rage, conflict, uncompromising rivalry, aggression toward women and children, other cultures and races; or an intropunitive one, a deadly depression with no exit in sight.

XVI. One of the things T. S. Eliot describes in his 1925 poem *The Hollow Men* is this deadly depression:

> We are the hollow men
> We are the stuffed men
> Leaning together
> Headpiece filled with straw. Alas!
> Our dried voices, when
> We whisper together
> Are quiet and meaningless
> As wind in dry grass
> or rats' feet over broken glass
> In our dry cellar

XVII. Timid, full of fear of death, but pathetically reproducing the images of death (the 'other kingdom') over and over in mortal dread. The banal aesthetics of being stranded in the purgatory. Being able to move, but incapable of *passage a l'acte*; being able to have an idea and but unable to deal with its reality; being able to desire but unable to pursue it to the end. Our deadly depression has established its kingdom in this rift.

XVIII. We should also remember, though, that the same poem had 'Mistah Kurtz, he dead!' as an epithet, a reference to Joseph Conrad's *Heart of Darkness* (1899). That novel tells of the European white male plummeting into the heart of Black Africa to escape (what?), and finding himself there as well. A mixture of outrageous megalomania and an incredible sense of impotence paralyse the novel's protagonist, Kurtz, so much so that he can neither get out of bed nor is able speak, when he is finally found by Marlow, the man who had been looking for him along the Congo River. The indigenous tribe members around the hut where he sleeps have already turned him into a god. Kurtz, who is deadly terrified by the dark shadow he sees in the mirror held by Black Africans to deify him; Kurtz, who can only mutter 'The Horror! The Horror!' as he lies dying in delirium, is also here, living among us. 'Mistah Kurtz, he dead!' / 'Mistah Kurtz, he God!': same sentence.

XIX. Woody Allen, a third great psychoanalytical thinker of the twentieth century, constructs a scene in *Annie Hall* (1977) that addresses one of our innermost fantasies: While Alvy Singer (who doubtlessly is the alter-ego of the director/actor) is waiting in the line for tickets at the cinema, the man behind him, a parody of a typical New York quasi-intellectual, quite boisterously tells his girlfriend his opinions about… everything. At one point he starts talking about Marshall McLuhan. At first, Alvy only joins the argument in asides directed at the camera, but in the end, he can't stand it anymore and tells the man he is talking bullshit: 'Alvy: Marshall McLuhan, you don't know anything about Marshall McLuhan!' to which the man answers in a high-handed manner 'Oh, really? Well, it just so happens I teach a class at Columbia called "TV, Media and Culture." So, I think my insights into Mr. McLuhan, well, have a great deal of validity!' Instead of an answer, Alvy walks behind the poster nearby and pulls McLuhan (the real McLuhan) into the frame. McLuhan turns to the know-all intellectual and says, 'I heard what you were saying! You know nothing of my work! […] How you got to teach a course in anything is totally amazing!' And Alvy turns to the audience and says, 'Boy, if life were only like this!' Don't we all want this!

XX. But unfortunately, this is just an infantile dream. A pure wish fulfilment fantasy, the absolute reference, the Other finally giving us an answer: The perfect orgasm. Aren't we all after this, all the time? But there are no perfect orgasms in real life; If you have the luck, like Woody Allen, or rather, if you are not a confused semi-intellectual, like Alvy in *Annie Hall* who is scared stiff of any kind of action, but a director who more or less knows what he wants (albeit as confused), like Woody Allen himself, you can (re)produce its representations.

XXI. 'When John Gordon first heard the voice inside his mind, he thought that he was going crazy. It came first at night when he was just falling asleep. Through his drowsing thoughts, it spoke sharp and clear. "Can you hear me, John Gordon? Can you hear me call?"' I read this in a book published in 1954 in Turkish; it didn't have the name of the author on the cover, no information about when or where the original was published, only the name of the translator, which proved to be an alias. When I read it in 1969, I was thirteen. I was able to find out the author and the original name of the book only in the '90s, twenty-five years after I first read it. It was *The Star Kings* by Edmond Hamilton, published in 1949. For quite a while in and after

1969, I waited for the voice 'Can you hear me, Bülent Somay? Can you hear me call?' before falling asleep. Zarth Arn would invite me to his time, 200,000 years into the future, to the Mid-Galactic Empire; I would accidentally replace him and become first the Prince, then the heir-apparent and eventually the Emperor of the Mid-Galactic Empire, and I would command hundreds of thousands of spaceships and conquer other star systems and constellations in a war that spanned the entire galaxy. I had already fallen in love with Princess Lianna. The voice never came. I think this is one of the reasons I still have trouble falling asleep, or, have what therapists would call 'a mild sleeping disorder'.

XXII. On the one side there is Shorr Khan (this is a cold war novel: Stalin? Mao? But definitely the big Other) and the traitor Corbulo; on the other side, there is me and Lianna, who is madly in love with me, listening intently to everything I say, ready to die for me. How banally Oedipal it sounds, when reiterated like that years later! The only club I will be willing to be a member of will never have me as a member, because it does not exist in real life. If I am unable to become the Mid-Galactic Emperor, what good is being the top of my class?

XXIII. Indeed, when John Gordon finally returns to his own time and job, he receives an offer to become an 'assistant-manager'. Here is his reaction: 'Gordon could have shouted with crazy laughter, the suggestion seemed so fantastic. He might be an assistant-manager? He, who as prince of the Empire's royal house had feasted with the star-kings at Throon? He, who had captained the hosts of the Kingdoms in the last great fight off Deneb? He, who had unloosed destruction on the Cloud and had riven space itself? But he did not laugh. He said quietly. "That would be a fine position for me, sir."' The urge to 'shout with crazy laughter' is our first introduction to cynicism. The following resignation and quiet acceptance that came later is how most of us make peace with the cynic within, which will endure for the rest of our lives (if we manage not to become professional cynics, that is).

XXIV. We are not absolute morons: of course we wouldn't have been cynics if there were a *deus ex machina*, a divine intervention that suddenly set things right, acknowledging and approving of us. If McLuhan jumped from behind the poster whenever we needed him, if Zarth Arn called us from beyond space and time, if we could really hear the revelation when we knelt... A lot of wishful thinking. We longed for McLuhan's sudden appearance, Marx's ghost, Freud's voice from the afterlife, a revelation that everyone could hear (preferably broadcast on television), after every discussion we lost (whether we succumbed to wicked rhetoric, or were ignored, being accused of the same, or were simply wrong). As we yielded to the bullying of an older and larger boy, we waited for the day when we would use the force that would 'rive space itself'.

XXV. This is the answer we give to *objet petit a*, to the object of desire: Megalomania and cynicism. *Objet petit a* is always 'then and there'. Nothing that can be done 'here and now' can ever satisfy that desire. Real needs and wants are dangerous. Because they can sometimes be satisfied and sometimes not, but never 'always' and never 'never'; the tantalisation, the feeling of having been 'shown but not given' will always be present. There is no such danger, however, in the *unattainable* desire. There is nothing shown, so it cannot be given in any case.

XXVI. 'Having been shown but not given.' The curse of Tantalus, stuck in the river, water up to our bellies and unable to move. When we bend down to drink, the water ebbs, when we try to grasp the fruit hanging from the branches above, they lift out of reach. Our biggest horror; the feeling that reminds us at all times of our exclusion, abandonment, jealousy and envy ('What was shown to me is definitely given to someone else!'). It is preferable to perish seeking the Holy Grail, in pursuit of unattainable desires, rather than dealing with this feeling.

XXVII. We are born into a family, inside an absolute, closed structure. We are committed to our mothers with an unconditional love; it will not take long for unconditional hatred to accompany this feeling. The father, who somewhat relaxes this absolute structure, brings at least some competition to this 'closed ecosystem', but it does not take long for him (in most cases) to settle into the position of absolute authority. The pursuit of the 'absolute' in adulthood seems to get stuck in these stages, especially the pre-Oedipal one. The way to grow up might be to give up the pursuit of the 'absolute', the pursuit of the object of desire that is never 'here and now'.

XXVIII. In order to desire the other, to compete with the other, to make love with the other, to hate the other, to feel 'envy and/or gratitude' towards the other, to argue with the other, it is necessary to leave the family hearth, where the 'other' is always confused with the 'I'. The pursuit of the absolute, megalomania, cynicism, all these are ways to cling on to the family hearth, to hide from the 'other' forever. Living in a womb as big as the universe, dreaming of a phallus large enough to move the universe.

XXIX.   Believing in this world, believing in God, believing in yourself. Pantheists say all three are the same thing, an integral whole. But every whole has an other. Therefore, I prefer to say, 'I am the one who is only whole when there is an other,' rather than 'I am God!'. Without my other I will fall apart. Psychosis is the only way to 'absolutely' reject the other.

XXX.   McLuhan will not come. Yet there are always possibilities to argue, to fight, to reach agreements, to talk nonsense, or make great, ground-breaking discoveries. Agreements will be temporary and mutable, nonsense is not final, it may contain profound insight, and the breakthrough our discovery has led to may prove to be a mare's nest three days later. So what?

XXXI.   If we find a club that will accept us as members, let's not miss it. Not in a cynical mood; not taking plenty of precautions in case of possible failure; not with a 'I'm here but my soul is elsewhere' attitude. Here and now.

CHAPTER 8

THE TRUTH IS OUT THERE/'THE REAL' IS OUT THERE SOMEWHERE

> Even if we offer our lives, as martyrs do for their church, this is a sacrifice that is offered for *our* desire for power or for the purpose of preserving our feeling of power. Those who feel 'I possess Truth' —how many possessions would they not abandon in order to save this feeling! What would they not throw over-board to stay 'on top'—which means, *above* the others who lack 'the Truth..!'
>
> Friedrich Nietzsche, *Gay Science, Book I:13*

I. The truth is always 'out there'. It never comes here, near us, where we can reach and grab it. It is outside. Sometimes we call it 'external reality', sometimes 'objective reality', sometimes Truth, sometimes just 'the Real'. Let it not come too close, let it wander aimlessly out there, outside, in space or in the other neighbourhood, beyond this river or that mountain, at whatever cost. Unfortunately, it is also Lacan's 'the Real' after all: the inchoate totality all that exists, which is beyond language, beyond comprehension, beyond meaning. Does it ever leave us alone, in our cosy self-assurance that everything is knowable, everything makes sense at one time or another, if not today, then definitely tomorrow? No. It always comes back to its place. And in case you are wondering, its place is nowhere but us, our very selves.

II. 'The Truth Is Out There' was the slogan for the TV series *The X Files* (1993-2002, 2018). The protagonist of the series, Fox Mulder is an FBI special agent assigned to investigate bizarre happenings ('the X Files'), and he is obsessed with the probable interventions of the aliens, otherworldly civilisations in every weird case he comes upon. If he can't find it, he grudgingly settles for any old supernatural, extraordinary explanation. His partner Diane Scully, on the other hand, is a sceptical, honest-to-goodness Woman of the Enlightenment. All these aliens, werewolves, vampires, telepathic villains seem very suspicious and exceedingly 'unscientific' to her, at least in the beginning. But willy-nilly, in many of the cases they encounter, she has to play along with his partner, either because of the 'evidence' or her first-hand experience, and becomes a true believer like her partner as years pass.

III. Unfortunately, before we start talking about this issue, it is necessary to have a tedious discussion about terminology. The original slogan is 'The truth is out there'. First of all, we have to decide whether the producers of the show really mean 'Truth' or just 'Reality'. In English, German and French, this is quite an established distinction: in English, Truth/Reality; in French, *verité/realité*; in German, *Wahrheit/Realität*. It is almost certain that they mean the former, not only in the sense that there is some kind of 'truth' in all these UFO sightings and 'abducted by the aliens' yarns, but also that all these tall-tales may give us some clues towards a greater 'Truth' of the cosmos, that we are not alone, not the only 'intelligent' beings in the universe.

IV. Truth, unlike Reality, is something that cannot be experienced and perceived first-hand. It can only be achieved by reasoning, contemplation and insight; or, in a different vein, it can be arrived at by means of intuition, revelation and faith. When viewed from an Enlightenment/rationalistic perspective, what we perceive and experience are only phenomena. We can gather information about the facts; we can measure them, record them, compile and archive them. Truth, however, is what is behind (or beyond) facts. Once we have gathered and classified the facts, we can reach the Truth through reflection or reasoning on these. Or, if the Truth we are seeking is something internal, pertaining to our own minds or spirits, we can do the same thing through insight. From a religious point of view, on the other hand, the phenomena we perceive and observe will always leave behind an inexplicable secret. We can reach that secret only through revelation, or faith, through the word of God or of his spokespersons, his prophets.

V. In Oriental/mystical belief systems, in Zen, Daoism, Buddhism or Sufism, which did not go through a phase similar to the European enlightenment, these two paths are intertwined. In their case, however, God or his spokespersons do not intervene, and we attain that secret again through insight or contemplation. We find the 'true path', as in religion, but now we do this in our own mind, in a way similar to, but not exactly the same as, rational contemplation.

VI. Reality is the name we give to the phenomenal world. Although we think that it is independent of our perceptions, which can deceive us at times, even most of the time, and even if we call it *external* or *objective* reality, it can only be reached through our subjective perceptions and experience. 'Even though the blind can't see them, the stars are still there,' said Nazım Hikmet in his *Rubaiyat*. Although its shape, scope and meaning are open to speculation, it is true that a universe exists independent of our perceptions. It is not a 'Reality', though: it cannot be, because it is by definition 'independent of our perceptions.' We can neither perceive nor experience this information; Only through reasoning and contemplation can we be convinced of its existence.

VII. Likewise, the existence (or non-existence) of God, for example, is not a Reality, but a Truth. It cannot be reached or comprehended through experience, experimentation or perception. It can only be conceived through divine message, revelation or faith, or the persistent lack thereof. Miracles do not 'objectively' prove the existence of God. Yesterday's miracles turn into today's ordinary, everyday phenomena. Recently, reanimation units in every hospital do what Jesus supposedly did for Lazarus every single day. However, just as the narrated miracle of Jesus does not *prove* the existence of God, the secularisation of the same miracle does not prove its non-existence. God's Truth is either achieved through faith, or, if there is no faith, not achieved at all.

VIII. As we can see, the path to Truth is not one, neither is it linear. Then again, it appears that Truth is not only 'one' anyway. Different mental processes arrive at different truths. Most conceptions of the universe, Newton's scheme, the Kant-Laplace scheme, and today's schemes fashioned according to the principles of non-Euclidean geometries, Relativity and/or Uncertainty principles, all stemmed from similar rational processes. From the point of view of religion, Judaism, Christianity and Islam are all Abrahamic religions of revelation and share more or less a common mythology, but the Gods that Moses and Jesus preach are not really alike; Jesus' God is forgiving and kind, while Moses' *Yahweh*, is a much more vengeful, wrathful and punitive God, while Islam's *Allah* occupies the midway position between these two.

IX. What is 'out there', then, is really Truth, not 'Reality'. But while we're at it, let's examine the rest of the statement as well: Is 'out there' really 'out there'? In the *X-Files* universe, the 'truth', that is, the secret behind the series of uncanny events that are taking place in our old world is hidden outside, in space, in other worlds, in otherworldly creatures.

X. The habit of placing 'secrets' somewhere outside our daily lives is as old as humanity. Across this river, past yonder mountain, in the Orient, beyond Mount Qaf, in 'Black' Africa, in newly discovered

America, in the Wild West, on (or in) the Moon, Mars, the rest of the Solar System, Alpha Centauri, Andromeda... We are always looking for the secret of the uncanny that is here and now, that is *inside*, in the beyond, in *terra incognita*. We never find that secret as such, but we find other 'secrets' while looking for it: for instance, we discover America, reach China, find ivory, gold or diamonds. At the same time, we murder Native Americans wholesale, colonise China and India, enslave Native Africans. Although we cannot solve the problems in our own land, we discover and/or colonise and brutalise new lands; invent and establish new countries and export our problems there in aggrandised form.

XI. Isn't the same true for our psychic lives? Don't we always look for the secret of the uncanny at our homes or inside ourselves, somewhere else, that is, outside? Don't we always blame others, that is, people outside ourselves, our families or tiny communities, for the shortcomings on the 'inside'? Our individual lack (or at least inadequacy) of insight, our inability to contemplate on our 'selves' and our immediate environment is also reflected in our species' inability to look for the secrets of the world outside the world itself, in real or imagined 'other worlds'. Our insistence on looking for 'foreign conspiracies' whenever we mess up everything in our own country is another indicator of this habit. It is always the 'O/other' that is responsible.

XII. This will also end up (as we will see further on) in the expectation of emancipation and salvation from the outside, either from a distant god, or from infinitely wise and benevolent 'aliens'

XIII. The Western genre was one of the obsessions of popular American literature and later cinema. Just as medieval Europe managed to create a figure of the romantic hero from the so-called knights, the stray packs of unemployed petty nobles whose only talent was to wear a heavy and bulky armour, carry swords and lances, and ride horses, American culture created a similar romantic hero from its own cattle herders. The armour was discarded, the sword and the lance turned into six-shooters, but the horse remained the same. The common point between the knight and the cowboy is that, in addition to riding a horse and using weapons, they both set sail to an unknown that no one (at least nobody *from here*) had gone before: the knight to the Middle East with the Crusades, the cowboy to the Wild West to discover new lands. Both were expected to cleanse these un- or little-known lands of the 'others' they encountered; the former of the Saracens, the latter of Native Americans, and open them up for colonisation. The former failed and returned home, only to prey on their own countrymen; the latter were victorious and disappeared, like all successful perpetrators of genocide.

XIV. As a matter of fact, a similar romantic hero was created even before the cowboys, based on the pirates of the Caribbean. These pirates, who were supposed to have sailed 'to the unknown' in their ships, were actually bandits, most of them mercenaries rather than robber-heroes, each one authorized by a specific European power to plunder from other European colonists. In the seventeenth and eighteenth centuries, European countries needed such bandits, since having large navies off the shores of the Americas was not yet economically viable. But 'going into the unknown' seemed so romantic to us that we created heroes straightaway from these thugs. In Gore Verbinski's *The Pirates of the Caribbean*, Johnny Depp's portrayal of the wild, somewhat effeminate, somewhat funny, somewhat reluctant hero, Captain Jack Sparrow, seems so cute that we forget that he is actually a very close relative of the rapists, plunderers and murderers such as Blackbeard, Jean Lafitte, William Kidd and Jack Rackham.

XV. In the 1960's a new kind of hero will be added to these, who will carry the idea of the journey to the unknown to its extreme: The Enterprise will start 'its five-year mission' to explore infinity (rather than split infinitives), 'to boldly go where no one has gone before'. *Star Trek*, a franchise that started in 1965 and is still going on full-force (as of 2020), in ten TV series and thirteen films, with many more either in production or on the drawing board, has proven to be one of the most resilient ideas in contemporary popular culture. It has achieved this by drawing its popularity from the insatiable sense of wonder into the unknown, into what is 'out there'

XVI. The Truth is always out there, where no one has gone before; in the beyond, out somewhere. Definitely not *here*.

XVII. In Stanley Kubrick's 1968 movie *2001: A Space Odyssey*, which made a big impact when it was first released, human history is told from the standpoint of a 'sentinel', an 'alien monolith' that was placed on Earth by an extraterrestrial civilisation, at a time when only humanoid apes roamed the world. Not surprisingly, the name of the Arthur C. Clarke story which was the inspiration and starting point of the movie, was 'The Sentinel' (1951). The monolith first witnesses the adventure of the hominids becoming *homo sapiens*, that is, the moment of their inventing the 'first' tool/weapon. Or, more precisely, like every supposedly 'impartial' observer, it becomes one of the agents of this transformation. Later, as civilization develops, human beings realise that more of these sentinels are also positioned in different locations throughout the solar system. Pursuing the extraterrestrial civilization that created and placed these monoliths, they finally find a way to open up to the universe somewhere beyond the orbit of Jupiter, even if not that civilisation itself.

XVIII. The Clarkian obsession with the 'Big Other', which we observe in most of his works, especially *Childhood's End* (1953), is the basic philosophical premise of this movie: Clarke constantly imagines and describes some alien civilisation that has reached such a high level in knowledge and technology, and, more importantly, wisdom, that it can act as a guardian, a benevolent protector for humanity.

XIX. Lacan, however, would have told Clarke straight away that there is no such thing as the 'Big Other'. We always yearn for a 'Father' in whose gaze we will be acknowledged and approved. It is not *our* real father, who usually does nothing of the sort, but an imaginary father, an omniscient and omnipresent one, who (over)sees everything we do, and we always judge our own worth through *his* eyes. We try to look our best in this big Other's Gaze and constantly crave for attention, recognition and approval. Not (only) because we are eternal children, incapable of an independent existence, but (also) because it is only through the big Other we can secure a place in the symbolic order. Unfortunately, however, the big Other does not exist, except in our fancy, so we spend our days paying homage to, and waiting for acknowledgement from a non-existent power, a name, an imaginary magnifying mirror of our own creation.

XX. Opening up to the universe, experiencing and recognising the perfect completeness of existence, feeling one with it. Isn't this what we've been after from the early days of what we call 'philosophy' anyway?

XXI. I mentioned the sixth stanza of Nâzım Hikmet's *Rubaiyat* above. Now let me try to examine that stanza, together with the three stanzas immediately following it.

> 6. She kissed me and said, 'These are my lips, real as the universe.'
> Said, 'You did not invent this fragrance, it's the spring evaporating in my hair,'
> Said, 'Whether you behold them in the sky or in my eyes,
> Even though the blind can't see them, the stars are still there.'

> 7. This garden, this damp earth, this scent of jasmine, this moonlit night,
> Will remain alight after I am gone

For it was there before me and also after I arrived, independently,
And it was only the semblance of this provenance projected on me

8. One day mother nature will call it quits, saying
   'The time of laughing and crying is over, my child…'
   And thus will commence again in all its immensity,
   Life, unseeing, unspeaking, unthinking life…

9. Day by day the parting draws near,
   Farewell dear old world
   And u n i v e r s e
   Well met.

XXII. Stanzas 6 and 7 tell us about 'objective reality'. The reality that will continue to exist, no matter whether we exist or not, whether we are there to perceive it. So far, it is possible to say that Nâzım maintains the traditional materialist attitude and upholds the classical materialist debate against the idealist doctrine that sees existence as a function of the human mind, or reason, or spirit, or will.

XXIII. However, in the 8th and 9th stanzas, Nâzım leaves this line of reasoning, taking a step forward rather than 'deviating' form his materialist stance, and questions the station and destiny of the subject that he had previously 'suspended' in order to substantiate the existence of objective reality. Objective reality does exist, but what about the subject that perceives it, the subject who names it 'objective reality'? Nâzım's answer to this is *death*. Death will open the pathway to unity with the universe, with the totality of existence. But didn't we know that anyway? Didn't Yunus Emre tell us the same thing six centuries before Nâzım, when he said 'What does die is just the flesh / Souls are not likely to perish'?

XXIV. Are the subject that greets the universe and the one saying goodbye to 'dear old world' the same? In Yunus, the 'goodbye' belongs to the flesh and the 'well-met' to the soul, so we can understand that he is talking about two separate subjects. In Nâzım, who is not a mystical poet at all, or at least whose mystical side we hadn't seen until the *Rubaiyat*, it is difficult to talk about such a strict separation. The real question is, however, whether it is possible for the subject who writes poetry, falls in love, eats, is imprisoned, fights, quarrels, betrays, is betrayed, laughs and cries, to meet the universe face to face, while still preserving the status of being a subject. Is it really possible to become one with 'unseeing, unspeaking, unthinking life' without sacrificing subjecthood, the sense of self and the capacity to act as such?

XXV. In another time, in another culture, Percy Bysshe Shelley, also a materialist poet, had told us a very similar story. In a lament written in 1821 on the untimely death of his dear friend John Keats, he suggested that death was actually a way of becoming One with the universe:

> The One remains, the Many change and pass
> Heaven's light forever shines, Earth's shadows fly
> Life like a dome of many-coloured glass
> Stains the white radiance of Eternity
> Until Death tramples it to fragments […]
> P. B. Shelley, *Adonais*, 52

XXVI. The truth is out there, but it seems that there is no way to reach it without dying; at least this is what our poets tell us: What 'philosophy' as we know it has been pursuing since its early days, is to perceive and understand the universe in its entirety. What mystics (and poets, even when they are not mystical) tell us is that, this is possible, but we must give up our lives for it; that is, we should sacrifice the *subject* who wonders about the totality of the universe in order to perceive it.

XXVII. We will only be able to get an answer to the question we could not ask (anymore).

XXVIII. There are two (actually three, since two always makes three) ways to do this. The first is to die. Being one with the universe, getting rid of the body and of the subject-mind. Unfortunately, we cannot provide evidence of this, because until now, there has not been anybody who has come back from death and told us what it is like to be one with the universe, to attain the truth of the universe. We can still *believe* (belief doesn't need proof) and say, like Camus, 'There's only one really serious philosophical problem, and that is suicide.'

XXIX. Or we can choose to remain mute, not to ask questions, not to provide answers; total silence. This is the path many mystics ultimately discover. Zen Masters are famous for not answering the questions their apprentices ask them. Ursula K. Le Guin, whom we know to be on good terms with Eastern philosophical thinking such as Zen and Daoism, creates a conversation between Arren, the future King of Enlad, and the Archmage Ged in *Earthsea*'s third book, *The Farthest Shore,* which, of course, is concerned with death and mortality:

> In the afternoon as they lazed under the awning rigged to give shelter from the imperious sun, Arren asked, 'What do we seek in Lorbanery?'
> That which we seek,' said Sparrowhawk.
> 'In Enlad,' said Arren after a while, 'we have a story about the boy whose schoolmaster was a stone.'
> 'Aye?... What did he learn?'
> 'Not to ask questions.'
> Ursula Le Guin, *The Farthest Shore*

Zen tells us that truth is something attainable, but none of the ways to attain it is hidden in the wise words your teacher or master may feed you. You reach for it yourself, and once after you achieve it, you cannot tell it to anyone else. Truth leaves the domain of language, the semiotic universe from the moment you reach it. It can only be meaningful as an experience of the body/soul (or the body/mind), not as a verbal or mental expression. At that exact moment, however, it loses its relation with the concept of 'meaning'.

XXX. Was this not also the last word of Ludwig Wittgenstein, who reached a similar conclusion through a 'Western' mode of reasoning rather than an 'Oriental' one, such as Zen, Daoism or Sufism: '*Wovon man nicht sprechen kann, darüber muss man schweigen*': 'One should keep quiet on what he cannot talk about.' (Wittgenstein 1921/1974, *Tractatus Logico-Philosophicus*, 7)

XXXI. We talked about two ways to 'get to the Truth'. So what could be the third way hidden in these two? Such a way that will include both but will be neither, negate both but retain both?

XXXII. Both of these ways have a common feature, or a common *defect*. In both ways, the ones who 'attain the Truth', are radically separated from the rest of humanity who cannot, and become unable to establish a relationship with them. In the former, because they are dead and have abandoned the world of mortals, and in the latter because they have left the domain of language, the semiotic cosmos.

XXXIII. Although Zen, Daoism, Sufism and Buddhism are thought systems ethically and morally built on modesty and acceptance, they still cannot avoid a kind of elitism and arrogance at this point, albeit inadvertently: the ones who attain the Truth irreversibly transcend to another level. This may not be such a banal presumption as the prophets and leaders of these end times who proclaim 'I possess the

Truth, all of you, ignore the facts and follow me!', but they still divide humanity into a minority that has access to the Truth and a majority that does not. Which is exactly the same division that Marx describes in his *Theses on Feuerbach*:

> 3. The question whether objective truth can be attributed to human thinking is not a question of theory but is a *practical* question. Man must prove the truth, i.e., the reality and power, the this-worldliness of his thinking in practice. dispute over the reality or non-reality of thinking which is isolated from practice is a purely *scholastic* question.

> 4. The materialist doctrine concerning the changing of circumstances and upbringing forgets that circumstances are changed by men and that the educator must himself be educated. This doctrine must, therefore, divide society into two parts, one of which is superior to society.
> The coincidence of the changing of circumstances and of human activity can be conceived and rationally understood only as revolutionary practice.

XXXIV. Truth can be in death, or it can be in the trans-semiotic space (*Fenafillah* [the transcendental plane of existence in Sufism]? Nirvana?) available only to the mystic who disciplines his body/soul/mind. But if we are looking for a transmissible Truth that can have a real value in our lives and during our lifetimes, we must not forget that 'revolutionary practice' too, in the true sense of the term, actually begins where language ends.

XXXV. The Truth, which can protect us from perceiving 'the Real' as an image of horror, which appears to us elusively, indefinably, from the corner of our eyes, through the cracks and gaps of the symbolic order, and freezing us solid like all mythological characters who encounter the Real face to face, is nothing but this revolutionary practice.

INDEX

Allen, Woody, *Bananas* (1971), 1.2-10, 1.37-44, 5.27; 'Viva Vargas' (in *Getting Even*, 1971), 1.41; *Annie Hall* (1977), 1.9, 7.19.
Almodóvar, Pedro, *Todo sobre mi madre* (All About My Mother, 1999), 4.15, 4.19.
Angel (1999-2004), 5.45.
Aragon, Louis, '*Il n'y a pas d'amour heureux;*' (1944), 5.38.
Asena, Duygu, *Kadının Adı Yok* (The Woman Has No Name, 1987), 6.1, 6.40.
Bataille, Georges / Christophe Honoré, *Ma Mère* (My Mother, 1966/2004), 6.23.
Berdyaev, Nikolai, 3.52.
Boorman, John, *Excalibur* (1981), 2.15, 2.20.
Brecht, Bertolt, *An die Nachgeborenen* (1939), 3.21.
Buñuel, Luis, *Cet obscur objet du désir* (That Dark/Obscure Object of Desire, 1977), 4.6, 4.11, 4.15; *Belle du jour* (1967), 4.11.
Butler, Judith, 2.29.
Calvino, Italo, *Il Cavaliere Inesistente* (The Non-Existent Knight, 1959), 2.22, 2.26.
Camus, Albert, 8.28.
Castro, Fidel, 1.40.
Cervantes, Miguel, *Don Quixote* (1605-15), 2.8
Clarke, Arthur C., 'The Sentinel' (1951), 8.13; *Childhood's End* (1953), 8.17
Cohen, Leonard, *I Tried to Leave You* (1974), 1.34; *Sisters of Mercy* (1967), 3, *Anthem* 1992), 6.42.
Conrad, Joseph, *Heart of Darkness* (1899), 7.16
de Gouges, Olympe, *Déclaration des droits de la femme et de la citoyenne* (Declaration of the Rights of the Woman and the [Female] Citizen, 1791), 6.38-9.
Dostoevsky, Fyodor, *Notes from Underground* (1864), 7.
Doyle, A. Conan, *A Scandal in Bohemia* (1891), 6.
Dylan, Bob, *It Ain't Me Babe* (1964), 2
Eliot, T. S., *The Hollow Men* (1925), 7.16.
Freud, Sigmund, 6.13, 6.21, 6.47, 7.24.
Game of Thrones, The (novel [George R.R. Martin], 1996, TV series 2011-2019), 2.10.
Gilliam, Terry, *The Imaginarium of Doctor Parnassus* (2009), 4.10.

Gunn, James, *The Listeners* (1968;1972), 7.2
Hamilton, Edmond, *Star Kings* (1949), 7.21-3.
Hitchcock, Alfred, *Psycho* (1960), 3.42, 6.28; *Suspicion* (1941), 4.2; *Vertigo* (1958), 4.3.
Hite, Shere, (2004) [1976], *The Hite Report: A Nationwide Study of Female Sexuality*. New York, N.Y.: Seven Stories Press; 1.33.
Honoré, Christophe / Georges Bataille, *Ma Mère* (My Mother 2004/1966), 6.23.
Irigaray, Luce, 6.46.
Jackson, Peter / J. R. R. Tolkien, *The Lord of the Rings, The Return of the King* (1955/2003), 1.15
Kant, Immanuel, *The Science of Right* (1790), 5.
Kazan, Elia / Tennessee Williams, *A Streetcar Named Desire* (1947/1951), 4.15-6, 4.21.
King James Bible, 4.35-7, 6.16-7.
Kinsey Report, The; Kinsey, A., Pomeroy, W., Martin, C. & Gebhard, P. (1953); *Sexual Behavior in the Human Female*, Philadelphia: Saunders, 1.33.
Kubrick, Stanley, *2001: A Space Odyssey*, 8.17.
Lacan, Jacques, 4.27, 5.37, 6.2-5, 6.39, 6.41, *Seminar XII* (1964-5), 5.39, *Feminine Sexuality* (1982), 6.47.
La Déclaration universelle des droits de l'homme (Universal Declaration of the Rights of Man, 1789), 6.9, 6.38.
Le Guin, Ursula K., *The Farthest Shore* (1972), 8.29
Lem, Stanislaw, *Solaris* (1961), 7.4, 7.6.
McLuhan, Marshall, 7.19, 7.25.
Masters and Johnson Report, Masters, W.H.; Johnson, V.E. (1966); *Human Sexual Response*, New York: Bantam Books, 1.33.
Marvell, Andrew, *To His Coy Mistress* (1681), 2.38
Marx, Groucho, 7.13.
Marx, Karl, *Theses on Feuerbach* (1845), 8.33.
Marx, Karl and Friedrich Engels, *The German Ideology* (1844), 6.10.
Milton, John, *Paradise Lost* (1674), 6.22.
Nâzım Hikmet, *Rubailer* (Rubaiyat), 8.6, 8.21-4.
Nietzsche, Friedrich, *Gay Science* (1882), 8.

Index

Pasolini, Pier Paolo, *Teorema* (Theorem, 1968), 4.15, 4.20.
Petersen, Wolfgang, *Troy* (2004), 2.30.
Phillips, Adam, *Monogamy* (1996), 3.8, 5.5, 5.26, 5.43, 7.13.
Plato, 5.18.
Shakespeare, William, *Macbeth*, 1.14.
Shelley, Percy Bysshe, *Adonais* (1821), 8.25.
Sophocles, *Oedipus Tyrannus*, 6.21.
Star Trek, 8.15; (Original Series), 7.14
Thackeray, William, *Vanity Fair* (1847-48), 4.
Tolkien, J. R. R. / Peter Jackson, *The Lord of the Rings, The Return of the King* (1955/2003), 1.15.
X Files, The, 8.2, 8.9.
Verbinski, Gore, *Pirates of the Caribbean* (2003), 8.14.
Williams, Tennessee / Elia Kazan, *A Streetcar Named Desire*, 4.13, 4.14
Wittgenstein, Ludwig, *Tractatus Logico-Philosophicus* (1921), 8.30.
Yunus Emre, 8.16

www.ingramcontent.com/pod-product-compliance
Lightning Source LLC
Chambersburg PA
CBHW050244170426
43202CB00015B/2913